The God-Shaped Life

The God-Shaped Life

Restoring Our View of God, Self, and Others

Steven E. Goodenough

180 Perspective Publishing
Salem, Oregon · 2025

ISBN: 979-8-9931628-0-5
Published by 180 Perspective Publishing, Salem, Oregon.
www.180perspective.com

Cover design by Steven E. Goodenough
Interior formatting by Steven E. Goodenough

Contents

Preface

Every person carries a picture of God inside their mind and heart. That picture may have been shaped by family, church experiences, culture, or personal pain. For some, it is a picture of a distant ruler; for others, a strict judge. For still others, it is a vague blur of kindness with no real strength. Whatever your picture looks like, it has shaped the way you live.

Over the years, I've seen how a distorted view of God inevitably spills into how people see themselves. When we imagine God as harsh, we live with shame. When we picture Him as distant, we live without hope. And when our self-image is damaged, our relationships with others suffer. The cycle continues, leaving people frustrated and searching for meaning.

This book was written out of my deep conviction that God wants to restore the way you see Him, the way you see yourself, and the way you see others. A healthy view of God brings healing to your identity, renewal to your relationships, and restoration that reaches into the physical, mental, social, and spiritual parts of life. God has already revealed His heart to us through Scripture, and His truth has the power to free us from lies that hold us captive.

My prayer is that as you read these pages, you will find clarity and confidence in who God is, freedom in who you are in Christ, and grace for how you relate to others. Living a God-shaped life touches the everyday moments of work, family, friendships, and personal challenges.

As you work through each chapter, take your time. Pause with the reflection questions. Talk about the ideas with others if you can. This book is meant to be a journey, not a sprint. Each step you take will help you align more closely with God's truth and discover the life He designed for you.

My hope is simple: that you will see God more clearly, see yourself more truly, and see others through eyes of love. That is the life God intended. That is the God-shaped life.

Introduction

Imagine a life marked by victory over moral struggles—a life filled with greater meaning and purpose. Envision improving your self-esteem and discovering the confidence to become a better, more authentic version of yourself. Picture having healthier relationships with your spouse, friends, boss, coworkers, and others in your life. Consider possessing a healthier mind that enables you to overcome negative thinking, along with a body strengthened by better physical health. Above all, grasp the reality that God loves you beyond your comprehension. Imagine living a God-shaped life!

I believe God created each of us with a specific design and purpose. Unfortunately, influences such as genetics, our upbringing, culture, modern media, and religion have led us to adopt distorted concepts of God, develop poor self-images, and hold inaccurate views of others. As a result, many of us live outside of God's original design and purpose. The repercussions of these distortions extend beyond moral decay; they damage our brains, minds, and every aspect of our physical, social, and spiritual health. Our perception of God, our self-image, and our views of others profoundly shape our lives.

This book will guide you in identifying false concepts of God, problems with self-image, and distorted views of others. You will learn where and how these distortions developed and discover the effects they have on your physical brain, thought life, emotional well-being, physical health, spiritual vitality, and social interactions with those around you. You will also be introduced to God as He reveals Himself in the Bible, learn how being a new

1

creation in Christ can transform self-image issues, and understand how to love others through the lens of God's love. This book will provide practical advice on how to know God for who He truly is, see yourself as God sees you, and perceive others through His lens of love. Additionally, you will gain tools to share this truth with others in a simple yet effective manner. This book will help you discover that you were created for a God-shaped life.

For years, I struggled with false concepts of God, a crippling poor self-image, and distorted perceptions of others. Despite being a "Christian," I often felt powerless to overcome life's challenges. Driven by a longing for victory over the sins that so easily entangled me, I sought to understand the Word of God in depth. I plunged into the mysteries of the Bible and quickly realized I needed support. My pursuit led me to Bible college, where I earned a bachelor's degree in religion. My thirst for knowledge pushed me further into seminary, where I earned a Master of Arts in theological studies and then a Master of Divinity in Homiletics. Eventually, I pursued additional postgraduate academic work and ultimately earned a Doctor of Ministry. Every step of this educational journey was fueled by my desire to know God and His Word more deeply.

Yet, despite all this education, I still could not find moral purity or a genuine sense of God's love. I knew the Bible more thoroughly, but I filtered it through distorted concepts of God. Those distortions convinced me that I needed to achieve moral purity before God would accept me—a moral dilemma echoed in Paul's words: "I am doing the very thing I hate" (Rom. 7:15). Though I was "saved" and assured of heaven, I lacked the daily victory necessary to face life's challenges. I was trapped in the sin–repent–sin cycle: I would fall into sin, feel guilt and shame, repent and cry out for help, only to fall again — "Wretched man that I am! Who will set me free?" (Rom. 7:24).

Then, through God's grace, my eyes were opened. I realized that my distorted view of God was shaping the way I interpreted Scripture. That false perception not only warped my self-image but also colored how I interacted with others. When my understanding of God was corrected, I discovered His love to be greater than I could ever comprehend. Through the riches of His grace, demonstrated in Jesus Christ, I came to understand that I had been recreated with the power to walk in victory. By the Holy Spirit, I was given the ability to see others through the lens of God's great love. This renewed understanding of who God truly is, who I am as a new creation in Christ, and how I am called to view others has transformed my life. I want to share that discovery with you—the God-shaped life.

If you find yourself struggling with a distorted view of God, battling a poor self-image, or unable to love others selflessly, then the message of the God-shaped life is meant for you. In light of the turmoil and uncertainty in our world today, this message has never been more urgent. Don't delay—the God-shaped life is waiting for you!

Chapter One: The Problem

I've often heard the charge, "The church is full of hypocrites!" It's a statement that stings because it hits close to home. The usual response goes something like, "Christians aren't perfect, just forgiven." For years, I accepted that answer…yet it never sat well with me. I mean, aren't Christians supposed to be morally set apart from the secular world? You and I would probably both shake our heads in agreement. However, in the statement, "Christians aren't perfect, just forgiven," aren't we granting license for moral failure and excusing the fallout to the pretense of God's forgiving grace? And beyond morals, where is the love that the Bible declares the believer should be identified by? Hypocrisy in the church isn't uncovered by moral failure alone—it is unmasked when love is missing. For, as Paul reminds us, without love, we are nothing more than "a resounding gong or a clanging cymbal" (1 Cor. 13:1).

When love is absent, all that remains is empty religion—a hollow performance that convinces neither the watching world nor the believer himself. True faith, however, is recognized by transformation, where the grace of God does far more than simply pardon sin; it shapes a life that reflects His very character. This is the standard Jesus set for His followers, and it is the witness the world is searching for.

Too often, what we see in the church is not transformation but moral conformity for the sake of social acceptance. This happens when people adapt to outward standards or behavioral patterns in order to be received and thought well of, hoping to gain a sense of belonging and love from the group they wish to be accepted by.

I have experienced it as a young believer in Christ. I came fresh out of the early 80's rock influence—long hair and leather jacket. I found a little Baptist church I wanted to attend. That Sunday, after the church service, the pastor came over to my house and asked me to never come back because of my looks. In other words, I was labeled as unlovable by a group of Christians claiming to be followers and earthly ambassadors of the God of love. Now, if I had cut my hair and changed my clothing, they would have been hugging me before the service even started. It was a clear reminder that when the church mistakes outward appearance for inward transformation, it forfeits its witness of love to the very people it is called to reach.

I wish I could report that my experience with that little Baptist church was an anomaly, but it was not. In fact, my experience with Christianity over the course of my life has left a bad taste in my mouth. If I had not had a strong commitment to truth and had not read and studied the Word of God for myself, I would have walked away from it all. However, and the opposite of walking away, my experiences drove me to want to bring change to the Body of Christ, not moral conformity—we've had enough of that—but real change in the heart and mind of the believer. A change that embraces and encompasses the truth of God's forgiving grace. Not one like a recent accusation I heard, "Grace to you Christians is a license to sin and still think you're okay with God!"

In fact, outside of the secular observations, Christianity is beginning to look in the mirror and notice something is wrong. I recently read a statement by Timothy Jennings, "There is something wrong with Christianity."[1] As I read this and Jennings' further clarifications, I realized that my ministry experience affirms Jennings' statement. I have often wondered why there are some whom I minister to that never seem to grow spiritually. They continuously struggle with the same problems and addictions repeatedly. It makes me wonder why it is so difficult to grow true disciples of Christ in our modern culture.

Even worse, it appears that our modern culture is doing a better job at making disciples than Christians are. The result is that nowadays Christians are just as morally corrupt as the world around them. In a recent interview with *Homiletics Online*, George Barna stated, "When we look at the values, lifestyles, the moral perspective, and behaviors of Christians, we can see that there's virtually no difference between Christians and non-Christians."[2]

Jennings' research validates Barna's statement. Jennings recounts, "Multiple studies document that domestic violence against women is no different in Christian homes than in non-Christian homes."[3] In fact, in some cases, it is more likely that a man will be abused by a Christian woman than by a non-Christian. Jennings goes on to report that in America, where the majority of us claim to be Christian, we have the highest rate of teen

---

[1] Timothy R. Jennings, *The God-Shaped Brain: How Changing Your View of God Transforms Your Life* (Downers Grove, IL: InterVarsity Press, 2013), 21.

[2] George Barna, interview by *Homiletics Online*, April 2000.

[3] Jennings, The God-Shaped Brain, 47.

pregnancy and abortion in the world, more than twice that of any industrialized nation, and as much as ten times that of some non-Christian nations. In addition, alcohol use, drug abuse, and porn viewing are the same with Christians versus non-Christians. Worry and anxiety are the same amongst the two groups, and each year, sexual misconduct and lack of fulfilling responsibility have greatly increased across the board. There are news reports of sexual misconduct and attempts to cover up within Christian organizations. In addition to the fact that Christianity is splintered into tens of thousands of different denominations and lacks unity, when the Bible says there should be unity. However, Jennings' most profound expression is, "Perhaps the most distressing problem in Christianity is distorted ideas about God."[4]

We can no longer excuse Christianity's perverted moral indulgence with the statement "not perfect, just forgiven," and just teaching them the Bible does not seem to create the spiritual growth the Scriptures say should happen within the faith arena. What is wrong with Christianity? If placing faith in Christ makes us no better than the world around us, is there any validity to it? The church has reduced herself to fit the label, "hypocrite." The Bible does not say that they would know a Christian by his hypocrisy. If there is validity to the truth of God's Word, then where has the church gone wrong? And what do we do to fix it? The problem is that you cannot fix something if you do not know what is wrong with it.

In this book, I seek to reveal what is wrong with Christianity and offer practical procedures for restoring

---

[4] Jennings, The God-Shaped Brain, 52.

the church to health. However, my intention here is not to criticize the church. While I do agree that there is something wrong with Christianity, I know that there are many well-meaning and good-hearted people in the church. I do not know of a pastor or ministry leader who does not have good intentions. I am sure there are some who exist for selfish motives and do not give a hoot about those in his or her care. However, that would not be the norm. Nonetheless, most ministry leaders have never been trained in how to make disciples of Christ. We lead potential candidates through a prayer and then baptize them. We then ask them to regularly attend worship service and possibly a midweek Bible study. The result is the new convert is versed in the dos and don'ts of church acceptance—as I said earlier, "moral conformity for social acceptance"—along with the particular church's doctrinal persuasion. Obviously, this is not working.

While perplexed about these problems and how to help those in my pastoral care to find victory over the sin that so easily entangles, I began to read and study discipleship strategies. One day, I read a statement from Bill Bright, who essentially said that in reality, every aspect of our lives—our attitudes, intentions, aspirations, behaviors, and even our speech—is shaped by our perception of God.[5] Whether we're facing financial struggles, moral dilemmas, or emotional challenges, and whether we're tempted by desires like lust, anxiety, anger, or insecurity, our actions are a reflection of our understanding of God. Our beliefs about God's nature impact not only our relationships and how we spend our

---

[5] Bill Bright, *The Journey Home* (Orlando: NewLife, 1995), 34.

time at work and during leisure, but also the kinds of books we read and the music we listen to.

Bright's statement was an eye-opener for me. I began to read book after book by well-received ministers and found that they all made similar statements. For example, Larry Stephens commented, "Our image of God has profound and definite effects on our lives, our relationships, and our personal psychology. Our image of God affects how we think, feel, make choices, respond to life, and relate to others."[6] A. W. Tozer revealed, "It is impossible to keep our moral practices sound and our inward attitudes right while our idea of God is erroneous or inadequate. If we would bring back spiritual power to our lives, we must begin to think of God more nearly as He is."[7] J. I. Packer wrote, "Knowing about God is crucially important for the living of our lives."[8] Charles Stanley said, "Nothing is more valuable than knowing God."[9] Norman Geisler stated, "To embrace false teaching, especially about God, is to skate on thin ice. It is dangerous to our spiritual well-being."[10] The list goes on.

I discovered that the first piece of the puzzle regarding modern Christianity's moral dilemma is her

------

[6] Larry Stephens, *Your Image of God Shapes You* (Nashville: Abingdon, 2002), 18.

[7] A. W. Tozer, *The Knowledge of the Holy* (New York: HarperCollins, 1961), 4.

[8] J. I. Packer, *Knowing God* (Downers Grove, IL: InterVarsity, 1973), 27.

[9] Charles Stanley, *The Wonderful Spirit-Filled Life* (Nashville: Thomas Nelson, 1992), 56.

[10] Norman Geisler, *Systematic Theology* (Minneapolis: Bethany House, 2002), 144.

view of God, which has a direct impact on how Christians live their lives, and particularly their moral well-being. Shortly after discovering the first piece of the puzzle, I read where a Baylor University study revealed that seventy-seven percent of Christians hold a distorted view of God.[11] Then I found that Stephens's research has revealed that eighty-five percent of professing believers in Jesus Christ have a distorted view of God.[12] The majority view God as either an authoritative dictator, distantly disengaged, or critical. Less than one in four view God as a benevolent, loving Creator actively engaged in pursuing mankind to restore fellowship with Him. The second piece of the puzzle came into focus.

As I contemplated all this information, I realized that if roughly eighty percent plus of professing believers in Christ hold a distorted view of God, which impacts morality, then the problem with Christianity is its view of God. Tozer warned of this several decades ago, saying, "The Church has surrendered her once lofty concept of God and has substituted for it one so low, so ignoble, as to be utterly unworthy of thinking, worshipping men."[13] Tozer goes on to say,

"A right conception of God is basic not only to systematic theology but to practical Christian living as well. It is to worship what the foundation is to the temple; where it is inadequate or out of plumb, the whole

---

[11] Paul Froese and Christopher Bader, *America's Four Gods: What We Say About God—and What That Says About Us* (New York: Oxford University Press, 2010), 45.

[12] Stephens, Your Image of God Shapes You, 24.

[13] Tozer, The Knowledge of the Holy, 6.

structure must sooner or later collapse. I believe there is scarcely an error in doctrine or a failure in applying Christian ethics that cannot be traced finally to imperfect and ignoble thoughts about God."[14]

There it is! A right conception of God is basic to practical Christian living. The reason Christians are just as morally corrupt as the secular world is that the majority have lost their correct view of God. Furthermore, I also discovered that beyond morality, modern research has also demonstrated that a faulty concept of God leads to general health problems, as well as an unhealthy physical brain.

Additionally, if how we view God impacts our everyday living, then we would have to realize that it also impacts our self-image. And as Zig Ziglar says, "As individuals, we will consistently act according to the way we see ourselves."[15] If that is true, then what kind of self-image would a Christian have to act as morally corrupt as a non-Christian? If Christians continue to have the self-image of "not perfect, just forgiven," then what kind of moral lifestyle will be present? My experience has led me to believe that with moral laxity comes guilt and shame, which controls the ability to think. "We cannot think clearly when we are guilt-ridden. In order for our judgment to work best, our conscience must be clear. Clear thinking can only happen when we live in harmony with the law of love, which requires removing distorted God-concepts and coming back to a true knowledge of

---

[14] Tozer, The Knowledge of the Holy, 7.

[15] Zig Ziglar, *See You at the Top*, 25th anniv. ed. (Gretna, LA: Pelican, 2000), 65.

Him," writes Jennings.[16] Clearly, a distorted image of God can have a dramatic impact on self-image and ultimately influence how one approaches a relationship with God.

If the dots are connected, then a clearer picture emerges to reveal that if someone has a distorted image of God and a distorted self-image, then it will affect social interaction. Just watch the latest news, and you can easily see that people are largely motivated by selfish and immoral interests. The sad part is, Christians are actively engaged with social interaction in a bad way—they are not distinguishable from the secular culture, and when they act out in socially destructive ways, the media is all over it. It appears that one of the results of holding a distorted view of God, self, and others is a lack of giving and receiving love and grace. David Seamands saw similar patterns in his practice and wrote, "Many years ago I was driven to the conclusion that the two major causes of most emotional problems among evangelical Christians are these: the failure to understand, receive, and live out God's unconditional grace and forgiveness; and the failure to give out that unconditional love, forgiveness, and grace to other people."[17]

So then, how we view God sets the stage for the play of life. The stage sets the hue of our self-image and how we view and interact with the other characters we encounter. If there is a distortion in how we view God, then our purpose and interaction in the play will be a struggle.

---

[16] Jennings, The God-Shaped Brain, 75.

[17] David A. Seamands, *Healing Grace* (Colorado Springs: Victor, 1993), 35.

Within the following chapters of this book, I will explain where distorted images of God, self, and others come from; what the effects (outside of moral laxity) are of having a distorted image of God, self, and others; a brief overview of what the Bible says about who God really is, who you are as a new creation in Christ, and how to view others through the lens of God's altruistic love; and then offer a practical strategy to set out on a path of discovering God for who He really is, who you really are as a new creation in Christ, and how to view others through the lens of God's love.

My hope is that as you discover the real identity of God and experience His great love for you in Christ, how much He has done to make you His own with a new identity, how much you can learn to love others through the lens of God's love, then you can truly experience a peace that surpasses all understanding, a new purpose in life, and have a hope that does not disappoint—a God-shaped life.

Chapter Summary

In this chapter, we discovered that the church is no different morally than the secular world around it. We discussed that the major reason most Christians struggle with moral purity is that they have distorted ideas about God's character, which leads to a poor self-image and destroys the ability to see others with love.

If this diagnosis sounds sobering, it is meant to be. A healthy vision of God is not optional; it is foundational. Unless we see Him as He truly is, we will never see ourselves rightly, and we will never love others well. That is why the most urgent need of the church today is to restore a correct view of God. This is the starting point of discipleship, the seed of spiritual maturity, and the doorway to genuine transformation.

The chapters ahead will explore how these distorted ideas arise, how they damage our hearts and minds, and how God has revealed Himself so that we might live in the truth. If we are willing to confront our misconceptions and let Him reframe our vision, then the hypocrisy, confusion, and defeat so common in the church today can give way to authenticity, clarity, and victory. The path forward begins here: knowing God as He really is. This is where healing starts and where transformation takes root. But to restore a right vision of Him, we must first understand how our wrong ideas formed in the first place. In the next chapter, we'll uncover the origins of these distorted views of God, ourselves, and others, and see how the seeds of confusion were planted long ago. Only by tracing where the cracks began can we fully grasp how God intends to restore wholeness.

As we have seen, our view of God profoundly shapes how we live, think, and relate to others. But distorted views of God do not appear out of nowhere—they have roots. In the next chapter, we will trace where these ideas begin, exploring the influences that shape how we see God, ourselves, and the people around us.

Chapter One Reflection & Discussion Guide

For personal journaling, small group dialogue, or ministry training

Personal Reflection

1. What part of this chapter most resonated with your view of God right now?
2. In what ways have distorted ideas about God shaped the way you see yourself?
3. How has your view of God influenced the way you treat others—in your family, friendships, or ministry?

Bible Engagement

1. Read **Psalm 103:8–14** slowly. What words or phrases stand out to you about God's compassion and patience?
2. In **1 John 4:16–19,** John describes God's love and how it drives out fear. How does this passage challenge or encourage the way you relate to Him?
3. Reflect on **Romans 7:15**. How does Paul's struggle connect with the tension you've felt between knowing God's truth and living it out?

Group Discussion

1. What are some common misconceptions about God you've noticed in the church or culture?
2. How have family, culture, or media shaped your personal view of God?
3. If someone asked you, *"Why does your view of God matter?"* how would you answer them after going through this chapter?

Want to go deeper?

Download the free companion journal at 180perspective.com/the-God-shaped-life-study for extended prompts, prayers, and space to reflect.

Chapter Two: The Sources of Distorted Images

Every one of us carries images in our minds—pictures of what God is like, who we are, and how others should be treated. These images are powerful. They guide how we think, what we value, and how we live. Yet not all of them are true. Many are distorted, and those distortions have far-reaching effects on our relationships with God, ourselves, and the people around us.

Where do such images come from? Scripture and experience point to five major sources that shape our view of God, ourselves, and others. The first is the Genesis account of the Fall, in which Adam and Eve accepted a distorted view of God. The second is the influence of parents or early guardians, whose words and actions leave a lasting impression on a child's heart. The third is culture, which encompasses the shared beliefs and practices of the society in which we grow up. The fourth, closely tied to culture, is the overwhelming voice of modern media. And finally, the fifth is the religion we are exposed to—whether life-giving and true, or distorted and destructive.

Each of these influences shapes the lens through which we see God and interpret our world. If they are healthy, they help us live in truth. If they are distorted, they leave us with broken patterns of thinking that affect every dimension of life. Unless God renews our minds, we carry these distortions into adulthood, and they become the framework through which we see and respond to everything around us.

To understand how deeply this distortion runs, we must return to where it all began—in the Garden of Eden.

The Fall (Adam and Eve)

One of the outcomes of knowing where something began is discovering what caused the problem in the first place and then possibly preventing it from happening again in the future. However, even with that said, there are some things that mankind has done to himself that cannot be corrected by his own resourcefulness, one of those being the beginning of his separation from God. Only intervention from God can fix such a problem.

The Bible says, "In the beginning God created everything, and it was good" (Gen. 1:31). Since everything was good, Adam and Eve's minds were healthy because they had a healthy view of God, a healthy self-image, and a healthy view of each other. Genesis describes them as "naked," open and without disguise. The Hebrew word here is 'ărummîm, which conveys innocence and transparency. In sharp contrast, when the serpent is introduced, the Hebrew uses a word that sounds almost the same but means something very different: 'ārûm—shrewd, crafty, clothed in cunning (Gen. 3:1).[18] Humanity was uncovered and innocent, while the serpent was covered in deception. From the very start, innocence was confronted by hidden motives.

The serpent engaged Eve in a conversation about a tree placed in the Garden of Eden, from which God had

---

[18] Gordon J. Wenham, *Genesis 1–15*, Word Biblical Commentary, vol. 1 (Waco, TX: Word Books, 1987), 72–73.

commanded Adam not to eat before Eve was even created (Gen. 2:16–17, 22). Eve had not been present when God gave that command, so what she knew of it was secondhand. Still, Adam and Eve had not eaten from the tree prior to this moment. Why? Because they trusted God and believed His warning about the consequences. The serpent challenged that trust, aiming to turn Eve's heart toward doubt and mistrust. God had a sincere interest in Adam and Eve's well-being, which is why He instructed them to avoid the fruit of the tree. God knew it would kill them. God loved Adam and Eve and did not want them to die.

The serpent's first words carried suspicion. In Hebrew he begins with the phrase *'ap kî*, "Really? Has God actually said...?" (Gen. 3:1).[19] It was not a neutral inquiry; it carried skepticism and challenged God's trustworthiness. By twisting God's words into a sweeping prohibition, the serpent exaggerated the command and accused God of restricting what He had given.

Eve repeated God's command but added something He had not said: "You must not touch it" (Gen. 3:3). She also softened God's clear warning, changing the strong "you will surely die" (*môt tamût*, Gen. 2:17) into the weaker "lest you die" (*pen-təmûtûn*, Gen. 3:3).[20] The text does not explain how these changes entered—whether through Adam's telling or Eve's interpretation—but the fact remains that her version no longer matched what God had spoken. In Hebrew, the shift is striking: God's certainty became Eve's possibility. That alteration blurred

---

[19] Wenham, *Genesis 1–15*, 72–73.

[20] Wenham, *Genesis 1–15*, 73.

the truth, and the serpent seized on it, answering with bold contradiction, "You will not surely die" (Gen. 3:4).[21]

As those doubts took root, Eve began to question whether God truly cared for her well-being. That questioning gave birth to a new belief that God was lying to her, forming an image of Him as untrustworthy. Her new perspective reshaped how she viewed the fruit—"that the tree was good for food, and that it was a delight to the eyes, and that the tree was desirable to make one wise" (Gen. 3:6). She acted on that belief by eating and then enticing Adam to do the same.

The result, among many others, was a change in Adam and Eve's very nature. I believe it was both genetic and spiritual. Adam and Eve were now mentally challenged in their ability to hold a healthy view of God, and they would struggle with that view for the rest of their lives. They handed down this distortion to their children, carrying forward a bent way of seeing God that placed humanity outside of His original design.[22]

Consider their first two sons: Cain and Abel. Cain struggled with the same distortion. His heart was unsettled, weighed down by insecurity and the sense that God had overlooked him. Instead of resting in God's care, he carried suspicion, believing that God was not truly interested in his well-being. When God accepted Abel's offering but did not look with favor on Cain's, jealousy began to stir. Rather than seek God for understanding, Cain let resentment take root. In twisted

---

[21] Claus Westermann, *Genesis 1–11: A Continental Commentary* (Minneapolis: Fortress Press, 1994), 241.

[22] Jennings, The God-Shaped Brain, 45.

reasoning, he imagined that removing his brother would remove the problem. If Abel was gone, perhaps then God would turn toward him.

But Cain's problem was not Abel. His problem was the same one that began in Eden: a distorted view of God, of himself, and of his brother. His offering was not rejected because God showed favoritism, but because his own heart was clouded by mistrust and jealousy. Instead of seeing Abel as a brother, he saw him as a rival, and he acted on that false belief.

Cain's choice became the first act of violence, showing how quickly distortion leads to destruction. His story reveals how jealousy twists judgment and how dangerous it becomes when insecurity drives our view of God, ourselves, and others.

It is obvious that Adam and Eve's view of God changed during their encounter with the serpent. As if that were not bad enough, their self-image was altered as well. Genesis 3:7–8 tells us that their eyes were opened, and they realized they were naked. They sewed fig leaves together to cover themselves, and when they heard the Lord coming, they hid. This was the first expression of self-consciousness and self-preservation, which continue to haunt mankind outside of God's design. When I say "the beginning of self-consciousness," I am not implying that Adam and Eve were not conscious of being human and alive. Rather, they became self-conscious in a new way—beginning to worry about how God saw them and how they saw each other. That same distorted self-consciousness has continued to surface in every generation since, shaping how people view God, themselves, and others.

Adam and Eve were altered mentally, physically, spiritually, and socially through their encounter with the serpent, and they passed those changes on to us. But God did not change. God continued to love Adam and Eve and all their offspring, including you and me.

Therefore, our spiritual and genetic propensity to adopt distorted ideas about God, self, and others began with Adam and Eve and was passed through their offspring, all the way down to our parents, who then passed this dilemma on to us.

Parental Influence

The second major influence on how we see God, ourselves, and others is the home. From the moment a child is born, the process of learning begins. God designed children to develop by watching, listening, and responding to the parents who nurture them.

From the very beginning, God designed children to learn from their parents. This is true in the animal kingdom as well as among humans. A baby giraffe, for instance, instinctively responds to its mother's nudging to stand shortly after birth. Within minutes, that wobbly calf finds its legs, because survival depends on it. Human children are no different in their design to learn. They watch, they listen, and they imitate. This God-given programming is powerful, and it shapes not only how we acquire skills but also how we learn to trust and relate to others.

I remember watching a documentary of a mother polar bear emerging from her den with two cubs. It was their first glimpse of the outside world. They frolicked in the snow, tumbling and playing, but their eyes never strayed far from their mother. When she broke through the ice to hunt for food, they eventually tried to mimic her movements. The mother never sat them down for a formal lesson, yet she was teaching them. By simply living, she modeled survival, and her cubs absorbed it.

In humans, this design extends beyond mere survival. Parents are a child's first role models, teaching what it means to trust, to love, and to interact with others. Trust—an essential expression of love—must be established early. Without it, a child's health, and in severe cases even survival, may be threatened. Research in child development has shown that infants deprived of consistent affection and care often experience what doctors call "failure to thrive."[23] But when love and trust are present, children gain security, and they begin to imitate the behaviors and attitudes modeled in the home. Over time, these patterns shape how they see themselves, others, and even God.

Research confirms this connection. The Barna Group reports that 64 percent of Americans say their family greatly influenced their personal identity.[24] It follows that parents also shape the earliest images a child forms of God. Larry Stephens illustrates this reality: "We project our mental-emotional image of our parents onto God like a movie projector projects a picture onto a movie

---

[23] Harry F. Harlow, "The Nature of Love," *American Psychologist* 13, no. 12 (1958): 673–685.

[24] Barna Group, *The Impact of Family on Identity Formation* (Ventura, CA: Barna Group, 2017).

screen."[25] The reel is recorded in childhood—frame by frame—through repeated experience. Later, when we think about God, that reel is cast upon Him.

Timothy Jennings adds that the human brain is wired to do this automatically.[26] We instinctively ascribe parental traits to God. This is called anthropomorphism—assigning human attributes to God—and it explains why people often imagine God through the lens of their parents. If a child grows up with loving and affirming parents, it is much easier to see God as caring and trustworthy. But if a child grows up in a home marked by harshness, neglect, or emotional distance, it is much harder to believe God is present and good.

The effect of parental influence extends beyond our view of God; it also touches our view of ourselves and others. Consider the story of an orphaned boy raised by cruel caretakers. They constantly told him he was worthless, and in time, he began to believe them. His self-image shriveled, and his behavior reflected the lie he had absorbed. Later, a loving family adopted him. They affirmed his value and poured love into him, and over time his self-image began to heal. The cruel words had planted distortion, but love replanted truth.

Parental influence leaves a deep mark. It can set us on a path toward healthy trust or toward distorted images of God, self, and others. But it does not have the final word.

-----

[25] Larry Stephens and Jim Denney, Please Let Me Know You, God: How to Restore a True Image of God and Experience His Love Again (Nashville: Thomas Nelson, 1993), 14–15.

[26] Jennings, The God-Shaped Brain, 30–31.

Genetics and upbringing may tilt the lens, but through Christ, our minds can be renewed. In Him, distorted images are replaced with truth. We come to know God as He truly is, discover our identity as His children, and learn to see others through the eyes of His grace.[27]

Cultural Influence

To understand how culture affects our view of God, we must first establish what culture is. Culture can be described as the shared beliefs and practices of a people group that shape the characteristic features of everyday life. In other words, culture is the collective way of life within a specific time and place. These shared practices are rooted in common beliefs, something we will explore more deeply later.

From a broad perspective, culture looks like a school of fish turning in unison or a herd of animals moving together. When one turns, the rest follow in synchronous harmony. Culture functions in the same way, producing recognizable patterns of behavior that distinguish one people group from another.

What was culturally normal in one time and place may be unthinkable in another. In ancient Rome, for example, the toga was everyday attire. Today, in the United States, clothing trends lean toward Nike, Ralph Lauren, or whatever brand happens to capture the moment. Cultural norms change, but culture is constantly shaping behavior and values.

Art, stories, and traditions also reveal culture. Through them, we gain insight into what life was like for

---

[27] Jennings, The God-Shaped Brain, 45.

people in earlier times. Consider the Greeks during Plato's day or the Hebrews in Egypt and during the Exodus. When we examine Israel's history, one image stands out clearly: Israel often adopted the cultural perspectives and practices of pagan nations, and the result was devastating. God warned Israel, "Watch yourself that you make no covenant with the inhabitants of the land into which you are going, or it will become a snare in your midst" (Exod. 34:12). The psalmist declared, "How blessed is the man who does not walk in the counsel of the wicked, nor stand in the path of sinners, nor sit in the seat of scoffers!" (Ps. 1:1). Israel's history shows what happens when God's people absorb the culture around them.

This tendency was not unique to Israel. God told His people, "You shall not follow the masses in doing evil" (Exod. 23:2). Why? Because He knew the pull of cultural influence runs deep in the human heart. Paul later warned the church, "Do not be deceived: 'Bad company corrupts good morals'" (1 Cor. 15:33).

Subcultures exist within the broader framework of culture. In the United States, these differences are evident between social classes, between the North and the South, and among peer groups. I remember in school we had "Stomps," "Jocks," "Nerds," and "Heads." Each had its own dress, habits, and attitudes. To be accepted, you had to look and act the part. I gravitated to the group that made me feel most at home.

Johnny's story illustrates the same point. Johnny grew up in a small Midwest town, a good student and even class president. When his father's job moved the family to Chicago, Johnny suddenly found himself the outsider.

Classmates mocked him as "Country boy." Longing to belong, he found acceptance with a group called "the Heads." At first, their smoking and drug use repulsed him, but his desperation to fit in overruled his resistance. Soon, he was smoking, stealing money for cigarettes, dressing like the group, experimenting with drugs, and adopting their attitude. By his fourteenth birthday, Johnny was arrested for carrying a weapon and selling drugs. Paul's warning rings true: "Bad company corrupts good morals" (1 Cor. 15:33).

Proverbs adds, "Do not associate with a man given to anger… or you will learn his ways and find a snare for yourself" (Prov. 22:24–25). I know a young man who experienced this. He was, by all accounts, a typical and masculine individual. But when he began dating a girl who identified as male, he started associating with a transgender community. Over time, he began dressing in women's clothing, taking hormones, and rejecting any reference to masculinity. He once admitted to me that he knew the influence was changing him. Proverbs warns again, "He who walks with wise men will be wise, but the companion of fools will suffer harm" (Prov. 13:20).

Modern psychology has confirmed this reality. Linda Garnets writes, "Most scientists now agree that human behavior invariably reflects both biological and environmental or experiential factors… Whatever possible influence hormones and genes may have on the development of human sexual orientation, they will invariably be indirect and strongly influenced by the social environment."[28] In other words, cultural and social environment can trigger genetic expression and reshape behavior.

Consider how television and movies have shifted cultural attitudes over the last fifty years. Behaviors that were once considered shameful or immoral are now portrayed as normal, even admirable. What was once unthinkable has become acceptable, not because truth has changed, but because culture has steadily reshaped perceptions. This didn't happen overnight. It happened gradually, through repetition and normalization, until the values of society reflected what screens portrayed. Culture whispers its message again and again until it becomes the assumed reality, and unless our minds are renewed by God's Word, we too will adopt its distorted images.

Alexander and Andrew Fingelkurts confirm that culture shapes belief and morality: "Religious experience is not determined by environmental and cultural factors, rather it is modulated by them... Any cultural characteristic takes as a given the innate biological characteristics of the human. However, many of these characteristics exist as potential and can be realized only in interaction with the environment."[29] Culture doesn't erase human nature—it modulates it. When cultural triggers emerge, they interact with core beliefs and manifest in behavior.

---

[28] Linda Garnets, "Sexual Orientations in Perspective," *Cultural Diversity and Ethnic Minority Psychology* 8, no. 2 (2002): 115–129.

[29] Alexander A. Fingelkurts and Andrew A. Fingelkurts, "Is Our Brain Hardwired to Produce God, or Is Our Brain Hardwired to Perceive God?" *Cognitive Processing* 10, no. 1 (2009): 13–29.

Kim Armstrong describes Chi-yue Chiu's research showing how values and norms are shaped not only by conscious choice but by unconscious cultural context.[30] Heidi Keller explains, "It is the cultural emphasis on autonomous and hierarchical socialization goals that seems to result in this divergence in cognitive abilities and behavior."[31] In other words, culture influences not just what we believe but how we think and behave.

A study of identical Korean twins reared apart highlights this. One was raised in America in affluence, the other in Korea in poverty. Despite genetic similarity, their mental health scores differed according to the culture in which they were raised. Even their religious interests diverged—the Korean twins' mother had aspired to be a shaman, which shaped her daughter's outlook. The study concluded that while genetics influences traits, cultural context plays a key role in the expression of mental health and religious practice.[32]

All of this raises a question: Are we bound by culture's influence? The answer is no. Paul wrote, "So this I say... that you walk no longer just as the Gentiles also walk, in the futility of their mind" (Eph. 4:17). He continues, "Lay aside the old self... be renewed in the spirit of your mind... put on the new self, which in the

---

[30] Kim Armstrong, "The Power of Culture," *Observer Magazine* 18, no. 5 (2005): 15–18.

[31] Heidi Keller, quoted in Armstrong, "The Power of Culture," 16.

[32] Thomas J. Bouchard Jr. et al., "Genetic and Environmental Influences on Mental Health and Religious Interests: A Twin Study," *Journal of Personality* 69, no. 6 (2001): 931–952.

likeness of God has been created in righteousness and holiness of the truth" (Eph. 4:22–24).

Cultural influence is powerful, but it is not absolute. In Christ, our minds can be renewed. God gives us the power to resist cultural distortion and to discover who He is, who we are as His children, and how to love others in truth. As Hebrews urges us, "Let us lay aside every encumbrance and the sin which so easily entangles us" (Heb. 12:1). And as Paul reminds us, we are to "stand firm" against "the spiritual forces of wickedness" that drive cultural distortion (Eph. 6:11–12).

While cultural influence shapes our identities and beliefs, the role of media in this process cannot be overlooked. Media serves as a powerful conduit for cultural messages, often amplifying and distorting the values that we internalize. It has the capacity to both reflect and shape societal norms, impacting our perceptions of reality. As we navigate the complexities of contemporary culture, it becomes crucial to examine how media influences our thoughts and behaviors, prompting us to discern which messages align with our values as children of God. Understanding this connection allows us to better resist the pressures of media distortion, empowering us to engage with content in a way that reflects our identity in Christ.

Media Influence

The influence of media plays a critical role in shaping our perceptions and beliefs from an early age. The parents or guardians we grow up with, along with the cultural environment we are immersed in, establish the foundation for our understanding of God, our self-image, and our relationships with others. However, this process doesn't end with early upbringing; as we engage with television and the internet, the messages we receive become amplified, further shaping our worldview and reinforcing cultural narratives.

According to the A.C. Nielsen Company, adults in the United States spend almost four-and-a-half hours each day with live and time-shifted TV—that is more than half the length of a traditional workday.[33] This does not take into account the additional amount of time spent on the internet, gaming devices, or scrolling through social media. Children are immersed as well. Most American children spend about three hours a day watching television. Added together, all types of screen time can total five to seven hours daily.[34]

What does this much screen time equate to? An article on the website *Erupting Mind* explains that watching TV puts the viewer into a highly suggestible, sleep-like hypnotic state.[35] This provides easy access to the subconscious and is one reason why it is easy to fall asleep while watching television. The article continues: "The hypnotic effect is largely caused by screen flicker which lowers your brainwaves into an alpha state, a state of mind you would normally associate with meditation or deep relaxation. In most people, this occurs within 30

---

[33] A.C. Nielsen Company, "Media Consumption in the United States: Adults' Average Daily TV Viewing," 2019 Report.

[34] Nielsen, "Children's Television Viewing Habits," 2018 Report.

[35] Martin, "How TV Affects Your Brain Functions," *Erupting Mind*, 2009, https://www.eruptingmind.com/how-tv-affects-your-brain/

seconds, or within three minutes for very light and infrequent TV viewers."[36]

Because of the hypnotic effect of television and the uncanny ability of producers to inject manipulative content, *Erupting Mind* suggests that TV is "an excellent tool to program the mind. It provides easy access to the subconscious, reduces your ability to analyze incoming information, and ensures constant daily exposure via a physical addiction."[37] What more does the enemy need to destroy our image of God?

The article further warns that the main concern with watching television is the lack of control over what enters the mind. Some of what is seen may be good, but much of it may be destructive. Words and phrases are often crafted in specific ways to influence thought—whether political slogans, fear-inducing news alerts, or advertising catchphrases. These strategies affect not only our opinions about politics or products but also our views of God, our self-image, and our relationships with others.

Andrew Newberg adds a further caution: "We also need to discern how easy it is for people to implant false beliefs in others. For example, if you listen to the media news, you might think that there is tremendous controversy raging between scientists and theologians, but a stroll through many American universities will show that, on the contrary, a deep interdisciplinary camaraderie

---

[36] Martin, "How TV Affects Your Brain Functions."

[37] Martin, "How TV Affects Your Brain Functions."

exists."[38] In other words, the media can distort reality by amplifying conflict and suppressing harmony.

Psychiatrists have noted that media often produces "vicarious" experiences, where viewers actually experience the emotions of characters on screen. In some cases, these experiences can embed memories in the brain as if the events had been lived personally. I have even heard of young children exposed to adult media suffering the same kind of mental trauma as if they had been physically abused.

Wes Moore makes a similar observation in his article "Television, Opiate of the Masses." He writes that the lower brain regions "cannot distinguish reality from fabricated images (a job performed by the neo-cortex), so they react to television content as though it were real, releasing appropriate hormones and so on."[39] In other words, the brain treats fabricated stories as lived reality.

The effects of media are not confined to entertainment. Many journal articles have documented how public views of LGBTQ issues shifted from hostility to tolerance, to acceptance, and now to endorsement—largely due to strategies implemented through entertainment media. Other reports have shown how political agendas are normalized through selective news coverage and framing. Violent programming has been linked to violent thoughts and tendencies. The more

---

[38] Andrew Newberg and Mark Robert Waldman, *How God Changes Your Brain* (New York: Ballantine Books, 2009), 85.

[39] Wes Moore, "Television, Opiate of the Masses," *Psychology Today*, 2010.

research I did on the effects of entertainment and news media, the more alarmed I became.

What is even more alarming is the imbalance between media consumption and Bible reading. According to *The Huffington Post*, only 9 percent of Americans read their Bibles daily, even though 78 percent identify as Christian.[40] Of those who do read the Bible, the average time spent is only fifteen minutes a day. By contrast, the average American spends five to seven hours daily consuming secular entertainment or news media. The question then becomes: Which has the greater influence on our lives—modern media or the Word of God?

It appears that modern media in its many forms is discipling America. Jesus said, "Everyone, after he has been fully trained, will be like his teacher" (Luke 6:40, NASB). Modern media works on altering our core beliefs, feeding us false images of God, false self-images, and distorted views of others. It erodes morality by blurring the lines between right and wrong. It trains us to believe and behave like what we are watching—a society without God.

The prophet Isaiah's words read as though they were written for our day:

> *"He who walks righteously and speaks with sincerity,*
> *He who rejects unjust gain*
> *And shakes his hands so that they hold no bribe;*
> *He who stops his ears from hearing about bloodshed*
> *And shuts his eyes from looking upon evil;*
> *He will dwell on the heights,*

---

[40] Huffington Post, "Americans and Bible Reading," 2013.

His refuge will be the impregnable rock;
His bread will be given him,
His water will be sure.
Your eyes will see the King in His beauty;
They will behold a far-distant land" (Isa. 33:15–17, NASB).

Notice Isaiah's warnings. First: "He who stops his ears from hearing about bloodshed." Modern news media thrives on reporting bloodshed, but rarely highlights those who demonstrate the love of Christ. Second: "He who shuts his eyes from looking upon evil." How often do we subject our eyes to evil through movies, shows, and videos? Jesus said, "The eye is the lamp of the body" (Matt. 6:22, NASB). In my early walk with Christ, I often failed to guard what I watched. I struggled with moral purity, repented, and prayed for deliverance, but then turned around and filled my eyes with more corrupt images. No wonder I continued to struggle.

Isaiah also promises blessings for those who turn from such influences. "He will dwell on the heights, His refuge will be the impregnable rock" (Isa. 33:16, NASB). The impregnable rock is Christ, and to dwell on the heights is salvation. Modern media will not lead us to see Jesus as He truly is, nor prepare us for His return. Only turning from corrupt influences allows us to see "the King in His beauty" and look toward "a far-distant land" (Isa. 33:17). That land is the Kingdom of God, fulfilled in Christ's return and in the new heaven and new earth (Rev. 21:1).

The psalmist prayed, "Turn away my eyes from looking at vanity, and revive me in Your ways" (Ps. 119:37, NASB). We must take control of what we allow into our eyes and ears if we are to regain moral clarity.

The answer is not in religion or mere moral discipline, but in turning to God's Word and God's Spirit, which renew our minds, restore our vision of God, and reshape our self-image and relationships.

As we step back and consider the influence of media, it becomes clear that it is not the only voice shaping how we see ourselves, others, and God. Media certainly has the power to distort, but another powerful influence runs just as deep—religion. The messages we absorb in religious settings can either point us to God as He truly is or cloud our vision with man-made distortions. Just as the images on our screens can bend our understanding of reality, the traditions and teachings we grow up with can either illuminate the truth of God or obscure it. To move toward clarity, we must take an honest look at how religion has shaped our beliefs and values, and weigh those influences against the truth of God's Word.

Religion Influence

Religion influences our view of God, our self-image, and how we view and interact with others. As stated earlier, modern research suggests that our brains are hardwired to perceive God. However, outside influences—such as environmental and cultural settings—do not determine whether we believe in God but can modify how that belief is expressed. In other words, religion does not establish the existence of belief but shapes the way we view the God we claim to believe in.

Andrew Newberg observes, "For the first few years of existence, we unquestioningly absorb the beliefs of others—parents, teachers, friends—to help us survive in the world. We assume, quite naturally, that what we are told is true, and these basic lessons of life become our foundation for building more sophisticated beliefs and ideals."[41] Jeremy Rhodes, in his doctoral research, adds, "The religious classifier most utilized in social science research has been denominational affiliation. Since Herberg's (1955) classic study *Protestant, Catholic, Jew*, scholars have come to believe that our sense of who we are as it relates to religious belief and practice is rooted in the religious communities to which we belong."[42] These observations point to the way religion lays the groundwork for our image of God, our view of ourselves, and our relationships with others. As we mature, exposure to parental influence, religious contexts, and modern media further entrenches these beliefs, making them increasingly difficult to change.

Newberg continues, "The brain is a stubborn organ. Once its primary set of beliefs has been established, the brain finds it difficult to integrate opposing ideas and beliefs. This has profound consequences for individuals and society, and helps to explain why some people cannot abandon destructive beliefs, be they religious, political, or psychological."[43]

If a strong foundation of faith is not laid early, however, it becomes easy to adopt the beliefs of others later in life—whether through friends, teachers, or modern media. Either way, the religious ideologies we

---

[41] Newberg and Waldman, *How God Changes Your Brain*, 34.

[42] Jeremy Rhodes, "Religion and Identity: Denominational Affiliation in American Religious Life" (PhD diss., University of Notre Dame, 2010), 112.

[43] Newberg and Waldman, *How God Changes Your Brain*, 56.

embrace will determine our understanding of the Bible and form the interpretive grid through which we process what we read. Dean Flemming writes, "Our cultural, sociological, and church contexts profoundly influence what we hear the text saying to us."[44] Once belief systems are formed through parental, cultural, and religious contexts, that interpretive grid will determine what we perceive to be true about God, ourselves, and others.

Yet even with abundant information available, misunderstanding remains common. Jim Wilhoit and Leland Ryken lament: "We live in an age of cheap and available information. Factual information about the Bible is readily at hand. But despite all the biblical information available, the church is often lacking in maturity and spiritual understanding, and its biblical illiteracy is often alarming."[45] Even when information is present, we often fail to engage. Or if we do read Scripture, we interpret it through a distorted grid inherited from parents, shaped by culture, and reinforced by religion. When Scripture is neglected, our view of God erodes, leaving a vacuum ready to be filled by someone else's ideas of God— whether or not they reflect truth.

I once met a man named Jim who illustrates this danger. Jim was convinced that any valid translation of the Bible had to be the King James Version. He even believed the original Hebrew and Greek were King James language. When I tried to gently help him examine his

---

[44] Dean Flemming, Contextualization in the New Testament: Patterns for Theology and Mission (Downers Grove, IL: InterVarsity Press, 2005), 17.

[45] Jim Wilhoit and Leland Ryken, *Effective Bible Teaching*, 2nd ed. (Grand Rapids: Baker Academic, 2012), 22.

belief, he became angry and threatened me. To Jim, I was one of those who had "wandered from the truth." Somewhere along the line, a pastor or teacher had convinced him that only the King James Version was acceptable. Jim never studied the history or transmission of the Bible for himself; he simply accepted what he was told by an authority he trusted. That belief became the grid through which he interpreted everything about God.

The result of all these influences is that we eventually form an image of God—whether accurate or distorted—and we begin to worship that image. Timothy Jennings explains: "By beholding we are changed. We actually become like the God we admire and worship. In psychiatry, this is known as modeling. This occurs due to the amazing ability of our brains to rewire based on the thoughts we think and the experiences of life."[46] In other words, what we worship is what we begin to resemble.

Rhodes discovered, for example, that "belief in a wrathful God is a significant predictor of intolerant political attitudes. They propose that when people believe that God is actively involved in punishing sinners (a belief commonly held by many Evangelicals); they will be less likely to extend civil liberties to political out-groups."[47] The consequences of distorted images of God can be profound—even violent. When someone bombs an abortion clinic in God's name, they act from the conviction that God Himself would do the same.

_____

[46] Jennings, The God-Shaped Brain, 122.

[47] Jeremy Rhodes, "Religion and Identity," 164.

This is why religion has splintered into such division. Religious persuasions and interpretive grids have given rise to tens of thousands of Christian denominations, each claiming the Bible as its authority. Jennings observes: "While many of these different groups argue over doctrine, ritual, and textual interpretation, perhaps the most distressing problem in Christianity is distorted ideas about God."[48] These distortions stem directly from the interpretive grids believers adopt.

But Paul gives us a different vision. In Ephesians 4:11–16 he writes that Christ "gave some as apostles, and some as prophets, and some as evangelists, and some as pastors and teachers," so that the saints might be equipped for ministry and the body of Christ built up. The outcome is "unity of the faith, and of the knowledge of the Son of God, to a mature man, to the measure of the stature which belongs to the fullness of Christ." Rather than being "tossed here and there by waves and carried about by every wind of doctrine," the body is meant to grow into Christ Himself. Doctrinal unity—not denominational separation—is Paul's goal. He sums it up: "Speaking the truth in love, we are to grow up in all aspects into Him who is the head, even Christ" (Eph. 4:15, NASB).

The call is clear. Leaders are to train God's people with the truth of His Word. The people, equipped with truth, build up the body and reach the lost. The result is unity, knowledge of Christ, spiritual maturity, and fullness. The primary role of pastors and teachers, then, is

---

[48] Jennings, The God-Shaped Brain, 139.

to present a clear image of God by helping people remove the distorted interpretive grids that obscure Him.

Paul's words in Ephesians 5 drive this home: "Therefore be imitators of God, as beloved children; and walk in love, just as Christ also loved you and gave Himself up for us" (Eph. 5:1–2, NASB). The word "therefore" here translates the Greek *oun*, meaning "accordingly." In other words, Paul connects this call directly to what he has just said: "Let all bitterness and wrath and anger and clamor and slander be put away from you… be kind to one another, tender-hearted, forgiving each other, just as God in Christ also has forgiven you" (Eph. 4:31–32, NASB). By forgiving one another and walking in love, we imitate God Himself.

In summary, religion profoundly shapes how we view God, ourselves, and others. It produces interpretive grids through which we read Scripture and develop our image of God. If distorted, these grids divide and confuse; if aligned with the love of God in Christ, they can unify and mature the body of Christ. The love of God revealed in Jesus should be the unifying center of our faith, drawing the church into one body that truly reflects His image.

Conclusion: Restoring the Image

In conclusion, Chapter Two shows that the images we hold about God, ourselves, and others carry profound consequences for our lives and relationships. From the beginning, Adam and Eve illustrate how trust in God's character was shattered when the serpent sowed doubt, corrupting their innocence and distorting their identity. That first distortion became the seedbed for every other influence we have examined—parental impressions, cultural pressures, the voice of modern media, and the shaping power of religion. Each of these can either point us to the truth of who God is or reinforce false images that lead us away from Him.

Recognizing how these distortions take root is essential for us today. Just as Adam and Eve questioned God's goodness, we too must confront the influences shaping our perceptions. When our interpretive grid is clouded by inherited lies, cultural values, media messages, or religious traditions, our view of God and ourselves becomes skewed. But through God's Word and Spirit, our minds can be renewed. By exposing the sources of distortion and returning to the truth revealed in Christ, we can untangle the broken patterns that entrap us.

The first step toward healing is acknowledging where distortion has entered. From there, we can learn to see God as He truly is, discover our identity as His beloved children, and begin to love others through His eyes. This is the path toward freedom, unity, and spiritual maturity—a restored view that leads us into the fullness of life God intended from the very beginning.

Understanding the origins of our beliefs helps us see why false ideas about God, ourselves, and others take hold so easily. But recognizing the source is only part of the picture. We must also face the consequences of holding on to distorted views. In the next chapter, we will explore how these beliefs impact our mental, physical, social, and spiritual health.

Chapter Two Reflection & Discussion Guide

For personal journaling, small group dialogue, or ministry training

Personal Reflection

1. When you think about your earliest impressions of God, what voices or experiences shaped them most strongly?
2. How has your relationship with your parents or caregivers influenced the way you see God?
3. Looking back, what cultural messages—through school, friends, or community—most shaped the way you viewed yourself and others?

Bible Engagement

1. Read **Genesis 3:1–13**. What stands out to you about how Adam and Eve's encounter with the serpent distorted their view of God and of themselves?
2. Reflect on **Proverbs 22:6** and **Ephesians 6:4**. How do these verses affirm the powerful role parents have in shaping a child's view of God?
3. Read **Romans 12:2**. How does this passage speak into the cultural and media influences we face today?

Group Discussion

1. What examples can you share of how media—TV, internet, or social media—has shaped people's view of God, themselves, or others?
2. How do you see religion—both healthy and unhealthy teaching—impacting people's perception of God?

3. If you were to explain to someone why understanding the origins of our views of God is so important, what would you say?

Want to go deeper?

Download the free companion journal at 180perspective.com/the-God-shaped-life-study for extended prompts, prayers, and space to reflect.

Chapter Three: The Consequences of Distorted Beliefs

The human mind is shaped by what it believes, and those beliefs impact every aspect of life. Timothy Jennings observes that what we believe about God changes us biologically, neurologically, relationally, and spiritually.[49] False ideas about God, ourselves, and others are not harmless misunderstandings; they can actually damage the way we think, feel, and behave.

When our beliefs about God are distorted, our relationship with Him suffers, our view of ourselves becomes unhealthy, and our treatment of others is diminished. These misconceptions are not merely theological errors—they strike at the very core of human well-being. They influence mental stability, physical health, social relationships, and spiritual vitality.

One of the most surprising discoveries for me in studying this subject was how deeply our view of God can affect our health as a whole. I had long understood that wrong beliefs could disrupt one's relationship with God, but I had never considered the far-reaching effects they might have. To realize that distorted beliefs could touch not only our spiritual lives but also our mental, physical, and social health was both eye-opening and sobering.

In this chapter, we will examine how false beliefs about God, ourselves, and others can negatively affect four vital dimensions of life: mental health, physical health, social health, and spiritual health. By exposing

---

[49] Jennings, *God-Shaped Brain*, 21–22.

these consequences, my aim is not to discourage but to underscore how urgent it is that we replace distortions with God's truth.

Mental Health

Quite often, when I am having a conversation with someone and I mention the fact that how we view God affects our mental and physical health, I usually get a response like, "I can see that" or "I believe that." Yet, I can tell by the initial facial expression that the concept has never been considered before. The truth is, there has not been much research into how our view of God affects us, and to a lesser degree, what research that has been done has not trickled down into the general population.

However, before we proceed, we need to define some key terms and clarify their meanings throughout the remainder of this chapter—terms such as "Brain" and "Mind." Jennings suggests that the brain/mind can be explained by comparing it to a computer.[50] I am going to follow Jennings' terms and want to give credit where credit is due. Therefore, the terms and their analogous description to a computer are Jennings' creation, but I have put them into my own words.

There are two different parts to a computer: the hardware and the software. The hardware is any physical component, like the hard drive or motherboard. The software, on the other hand, is comprised of programmed information—a series of instructions that a programmer writes and installs. The programmed information is read

---

[50] Jennings, *The God-Shaped Brain*, 21–22.

by the hard drive, resulting in a functional response by the hardware.

The brain is more like computer hardware. It is a part of the physical makeup—the composite of cells and cellular structures with chemical and electrical responses. We can open the skull and physically touch the brain structure. On the other hand, the mind is more like the software—the thinking part. The mind is not a physical entity that can be physically touched like the brain, but the mind causes the physical brain to react in a series of electrical and chemical impulses.

The mind is comprised of a combination of genetic predispositions and environmental influence. Genetic predispositions are natural tendencies or genetic expressions that are typically passed on through genes at conception. For example, a child may be more genetically prone to isolation because of discipline, while another child may tend to act out in anger under the same circumstances. However, in some instances, cultural influence can alter genetic expression. For example, altered genetic expression can happen in cases where a child is severely punished repeatedly for "acting out," and in response, the child's self-preservation mechanism kicks in or the natural tendency to want to feel loved overrules the "acting out" genetic preprogram, resulting in altered gene expression that is played out in more of a tendency to isolate. Yet, that is not the default mode. If left alone, genetic expression will typically resort to default mode, whatever that may be.

However, genetic predispositions are limited and only influence certain characteristics. As discussed earlier, a couple of identical Korean twins reared apart demonstrated genetic influence on antisocial features and aggression, among a few other traits. At the same time, environmental influence calibrated the Korean twins' cultural characteristics—such as cultural and religious expression, as well as language.

The environmental influence (specifically parental or guardian influence at early stages of development) supplies the "software" from which we operate or function within the cultural framework we find ourselves. This "software" is what I call core belief systems, out of which flow our values and the social interaction platform.

So then, depending on where you were born, i.e., France, Russia, America, etc., and the parental and cultural influence of that country, will determine what sort of software package you get. For example, if you were born in America, you will probably speak the American form of English and act "American" in how you live your life. If you were born in Korea, you would likely have a Korean software package, and you would speak Korean and act "Korean."

As mentioned in the Cultural Influence on Our View of God chapter earlier in this book, culture influences us heavily and quite often will determine our belief systems and subsequent values, and sets the stage for cultural interaction. Faulty information programmed into our minds can have adverse effects on the software or core belief systems, resulting in moral decline and unhealthy social interaction. Jennings says, "Our minds—our preconceived ideas, beliefs, and values—filter the data input and alter the outcomes of who we are and are becoming."[51]

Parental and environmental influence can implant negative thoughts, leading to distorted beliefs or what we might call "Viruses" into our minds. Again, to quote Jennings, "Just as a computer with the latest hardware will not function well if the software is corrupted with viruses, so too the human being with a healthy brain will not function well if the mind becomes corrupted with 'software viruses'—distorted and unhealthy belief systems."[52]

A virus typically disrupts or corrupts software functionality and, if not subdued, in rare circumstances, can have detrimental effects on the hardware. However, for the most part in the computer world, a software virus does not typically have a detrimental effect on hardware. For example, a virus can subdue the workings of the software package. Removing and reinstalling the software or running an antivirus program can eliminate the virus, and all the while, the hardware remains unaffected by the virus. However, this is not the case in the world of the living. A virus (negative thinking about God) will begin to corrupt the software (mind) and, if not subdued, will affect the hardware (physical brain) health. Jennings warns that, "Because the brain is changeable based on the beliefs, thoughts, and choices of the mind, faulty beliefs react back upon the brain, causing further negative brain

---

[51] Jennings, *God-Shaped Brain*, 23.

[52] Jennings, *God-Shaped Brain*, 24.

changes, and negative-reinforcing cascades can occur, which is one pathway of mental illness."[53]

The truth is, our minds are composed of belief systems, and as we have discussed earlier, our belief systems are developed through a combination of genetic characteristics and external influence. Out of our core belief systems flow our values, our self-image, and how we interact with the world around us. I have come to understand that the default mode for our core beliefs is a self-preservation focus, which we use as a filtration grid to interpret and process incoming data.

I will try to explain. We were born with the conscious awareness of our needs—a genetic preprogramming dilemma. For example, a baby will cry when consciously aware that she is hungry or needs a diaper change. The baby was not taught to respond this way but was genetically programmed to think and act along these lines. I do not believe this is what God originally intended. I believe that originally God made us not to be consciously aware of our needs. Our parents or guardians were genetically created to automatically care for us as infants and to demonstrate to us that God is also consciously aware of our needs before we ever were. However, that all changed in the Garden of Eden with the alteration of mankind's view of God. From that point on, and even though Adam and Eve were trying to be good parents (at least we can assume that), their distorted view of God left them with self-focused belief systems. In other words, Adam and Eve were not fully able to perceive their children's needs before their children were consciously

---

[53] Jennings, *God-Shaped Brain*, 26.

aware of them. Adam and Eve, though I am sure they meant well, were not fully capable of knowing beforehand what their child needed until the child cried, indicating that something was needed. I am not suggesting that Adam and Eve were not able to discern their baby's cry, but that they were not fully aware of the baby's need until the baby cried.

I believe Adam and Eve lost their ability to fully know their children's needs beforehand because they had become self-focused to a certain degree—something that did not exist prior to a change in their belief systems. This created a vacuum that altered the genetic makeup of their children as a way of adapting to their environment.

I am not proposing evolution, but from what I have come to understand, there are genetic alterations for adaptation. Not one species changing to another, but minor genetic alterations within species based on environmental factors. For example, antibiotic resistance. It has been shown that people can develop resistance to antibiotics over time, which changes their DNA. The children of the altered DNA parents have also been shown to carry the same resistance to antibiotics as their parents developed. If this is true, then it would make sense that the first children of Adam and Eve also inherited genetic alterations. Specifically, a change in their DNA that made them consciously aware of their needs— hence the crying to indicate that there is a need that the child wants addressed.

It is unfortunate, but the current state of mankind's belief systems has only exacerbated the problem. Through modern cultural influences like the media, we are constantly informed of our deficient state of existence. The fallout is that our self-image is damaged by the belief that we are in a constant state of needing something—a constant state of want. This sense of needing something more has genetically altered our gene pool, and we have passed that on to our children. This goes beyond a baby crying because he is hungry or needs a diaper changed. Our children are born with the preconditioned genetic programming of a false sense of need. It is in our genes to believe that we are lacking something—a sense of discontent. The problem is, Christians are not immune.

However, there is a cure. We can alter our DNA to be healthier by changing our belief systems. When Jesus was teaching a crowd of people, among the many great belief-changing statements that He made, one was when He said:

"For this reason, I say to you, do not be worried about your life, as to what you will eat or what you will drink; nor for your body, as to what you will put on. Isn't life more than food, and the body more than clothing? Look at the birds of the air, that they do not sow, nor reap, nor gather into barns, and yet your heavenly Father feeds them. Are you not worth much more than they? And who of you, by being worried, can add a single hour to his life? And why are you worried about clothing? Observe how the lilies of the field grow; they do not toil nor do they spin, yet I say to you that not even Solomon in all his glory clothed himself like one of these. But if God so clothes the grass of the field, which is alive today and tomorrow is thrown into the furnace, will He not much more clothe you? You of little faith! Do not worry then, saying, 'What will we eat?' or 'What will we drink?' or 'What will we wear for clothing?' For the Gentiles eagerly seek all these things; for your heavenly Father knows that you need all these things. But seek first His kingdom and His righteousness, and all these things will be added to you. So do not worry about tomorrow; for tomorrow will care for itself. Each day has enough trouble of its own" (Matt. 6:25–34).

Also, when talking about exercising faith and being patient when encountering trials James says, "So that you may be perfect and complete, lacking in nothing" (Jas. 1:4). Paul says, "We proclaim Him, admonishing every man and teaching every man with all wisdom, so that we may present every man complete in Christ" (Col. 1:28).

The idea of completeness suggests that there is nothing lacking; there is no conscious awareness of need, for every need is provided. If we were in a conscious state of not worrying about our needs but exercising faith, we would then be complete and lacking nothing. According to Paul, we are to, "Be anxious for nothing, but in everything by prayer and supplication with thanksgiving let your requests be made known to God" (Phil. 4:6). The result of exercising this kind of faith in God is that "The peace of God, which surpasses all comprehension, will guard your hearts and your minds in Christ Jesus" (Phil. 4:7). Paul goes on in verse eight to say, "Finally, brethren, whatever is true, whatever is honorable, whatever is right, whatever is pure, whatever is lovely, whatever is of good repute, if there is any excellence and if anything worthy of praise, dwell on these things" (Phil. 4:8). What Paul is describing here, and if practiced, leads to a change in the structure of our brains. In other words, if we dwell on the things Paul lists, then our brains will become healthier, which puts us in a better position to experience completeness. The result of experiencing completeness is a structural change in our DNA, which could be passed on to our children and, in turn, give them a greater chance of having the right kind of brains to navigate the dark waters of our current disgruntled world.

So then, even though our parents may have passed on altered genetic programming that caused us to be in a position of being behind the eight ball when it comes to conscious awareness of what we perceive to be a state of needing, we are not stuck there. There are things we can do now to bring about healthier structural changes to our brains in order to experience completeness in Christ, and we can pass the new genes on to our children. That is the purpose of this book.

What if our children have already been born? The changes in our brain structure will bring about a healthier attitude and outlook on life—a peace that surpasses all understanding. This will be a testimony to our children and others we may have influence over. If they see the positive change in our lives, they may desire to know what we are doing and hopefully follow our example. Yet, we need to remember to exercise prayer for them, and patience, and heaps of God's kind of love on them.

At this point, I want to give a word of caution. There are some who suggest that if there are any mental unhealthinesses among those in the camp of faith, it is due to demonic activity or an organic brain disease. It is not my purpose here to dispel or endorse the demonic, nor do I desire to rule it out altogether. As well, I believe there are cases where the physical brain (the hardware) can have organic defects that affect the mind's (the software) functionality. However, neither the demonic nor the organic is the norm. What I am proposing is that we can damage our otherwise healthy physical brains by harboring unhealthy beliefs and thoughts about God, self, and others. And by controlling our beliefs and thoughts, we put our physical brain and mind in a better position to experience health.

In summary, what we think and believe is heavily influenced by genetic and environmental data, which contribute to the thoughts we have about who God is and how we see ourselves, as well as how we view others, which will affect brain/mind health, for better or for worse. We can move ourselves into a better position of having better brain and mind health by controlling what we allow into our minds and taking every thought captive—renewing our minds in Christ.

Just as distorted beliefs can corrupt the mind and brain like a virus in the software of a computer, those same distortions do not stop there — they spill over into the health of the body itself.

Physical Health

Beyond mind and brain health, can our thoughts about God, self, and others affect our physical health? The answer is emphatically, "yes!" Negative thoughts about God, self, and others cause damage to the brain and body by activating the brain's stress circuits, which result in inflammatory cascades that, if continued for very long, can damage insulin receptors and increase the risk for diseases like diabetes mellitus type II, heart attacks, strokes, obesity, high cholesterol, depression, dementia, and other health problems.[54]

---

[54] Jennings, The God-Shaped Brain, 30.

This is especially true if you have a view of God as being an authoritarian dictator, which is how most believers see God. I struggled with this same sort of image of God for most of my faith journey. I kept thinking to myself that God was out to get me because of my sin. I was afraid of God, and out of that fear, I tried to keep Him at a distance. I did not feel that I was acceptable to God, even though I believed that I was saved by placing my faith in Jesus. I sought to morally conform myself to a "Christian" standard to win God's favor, but kept failing miserably—hence the fear of God. This led me to a sin–repent cycle. I would sin and have guilt and shame as a result, then pray and ask for God's forgiveness, and then complete the cycle all over again. I never found victory while holding the distorted view of God that I did.

In addition, my own self-image was very unhealthy, not to mention that I was not able to see others through the lens of God's love while stressed. Why? Because stress is typically a self-centered or self-focused response. This line of thinking brought undue chronic stress to my life. I had no idea of how my distorted view of God affected my mind/brain health, nor my physical health, for that matter.

In fact, our view of God has direct results on stress levels, as mentioned above in my own experience. However, a life lived outside of God's original design will result in chronic stress from a different perspective. For example, living a life of constantly sensing that there are unaddressed needs or the desire for wanting something more, among a gamut of other unhealthy belief systems, will result in chronic stress. Such is a life outside of God's original design and purpose.

Negative beliefs and distorted ideas about God, self, and others cause stress. The body responds to stress by going into what is known as the fight-or-flight mode. When in the fight-or-flight mode, the oxygen supply to the brain is constrained and sent to the muscles. Not only that, but neurotransmitters are sent out that bind with the receptors of the cells, which is a good thing at first, but if it continues to happen over a long period of time, it lowers immunity and can damage the cell permanently. Caroline Leaf observes, "It's a profound and eye-opening thought to realize something seemingly immaterial like a belief can take on a physical existence as a positive or negative change in our cells."[55]

In summary, how we view God, self, and others can have a positive or negative impact on cellular health. If we see God in a negative light, or seek to hide from the wrathful god we've been taught exists, and deny the real God's existence altogether, negative changes at the cellular level take place, and these negative changes ultimately affect our physical health. Correcting our distorted images of God, self, and others triggers the restoration process and puts us into a better position to be physically healthier.

The damage of distorted beliefs about God, self, and others is not limited to what goes on inside our minds and bodies; it inevitably shows itself in how we treat other people and in the quality of our relationships.

---

[55] Caroline Leaf, *Switch On Your Brain* (Grand Rapids, MI: Baker Books, 2013), 33.

Social Health

How we view God also influences our social health. The way we think about God, ourselves, and others determines how we interact in relationships. A distorted view of God produces distorted social behavior. If we think of God as harsh, unforgiving, and distant, we are likely to reflect those same characteristics in our interactions with others.

Timothy Jennings notes that if we worship a God of love, we actually change into more loving people, but if we worship a god who is authoritarian and fear-inducing, we become more authoritarian and fearful ourselves.[56] Research in neuroscience confirms this principle. Andrew Newberg and Mark Waldman explain, "The way you perceive God changes your brain, and this in turn changes how you perceive yourself, your neighbors, and your world."[57]

Paul addressed this same reality when he described how unbelievers live: "So I tell you this, and insist on it in the Lord, that you must no longer live as the Gentiles do, in the futility of their thinking. They are darkened in their understanding and separated from the life of God because of the ignorance that is in them due to the hardening of their hearts. Having lost all sensitivity, they have given themselves over to sensuality so as to indulge in every kind of impurity, and they are full of greed" (Eph. 4:17–19).

---

[56] Jennings, *God-Shaped Brain*, 35.

[57] Newberg and Waldman, *How God Changes Your Brain*, 6.

Paul highlights that wrong thinking leads to a hardened heart, and a hardened heart leads to corrupted relationships. When we lose sight of God's true character and design, our interactions with others deteriorate. We turn inward, focused on our own desires, which breeds greed, impurity, and relational breakdown.

On the other hand, when our beliefs about God are aligned with truth, social health improves. We begin to treat others with grace, forgiveness, and love. As John reminds us, "We love because he first loved us" (1 John 4:19). In other words, a true view of God transforms not only our inner life but also the way we engage with the people around us.

And beyond our relationships with one another lies the deepest impact of all — the effect that distorted beliefs have on our very connection with God and the vitality of our spiritual life.

Spiritual Health

When I use the word *spiritual*, I do not mean some kind of vague mysticism. By *spiritual health*, I mean that part of us which connects to God, gives meaning to life, and enables us to live in harmony with His design.[58] From the beginning, humanity was created with this capacity. Genesis says, "Then the LORD God formed a man from the dust of the ground and breathed into his nostrils the breath of life, and the man became a living being" (Gen. 2:7).

---

[58] Dallas Willard, *Renovation of the Heart* (Colorado Springs: NavPress, 2002), 65.

This breath of life is more than mere oxygen; it is God's Spirit imparting to man the ability to relate to Him.[59] John confirms this when he writes, "In him was life, and that life was the light of all mankind" (John 1:4). But because of sin, humanity lost that spiritual connection. Jesus explained to Nicodemus, "Very truly I tell you, no one can see the kingdom of God unless they are born again" (John 3:3). In other words, spiritual life must be restored through new birth.

Paul wrote, "Therefore, just as sin entered the world through one man, and death through sin, and in this way death came to all people, because all sinned" (Rom. 5:12). Later he adds, "For as in Adam all die, so in Christ all will be made alive" (1 Cor. 15:22). Without Christ we remain spiritually dead, but in Him we receive true life.

Distorted views of God keep people from experiencing this new life. If you see God as a tyrant, you may try to hide from Him. If you see Him as distant, you may try to live independently from Him. If you see Him as indifferent, you may conclude that life has no real meaning. All of these distortions damage spiritual health.[60]

But when our beliefs about God align with truth, our spirits come alive. Jesus restores what was lost in the garden. He reconciles us to God so that, as Paul wrote, "the Spirit himself testifies with our spirit that we are God's children" (Rom. 8:16). In Christ we receive identity, purpose, and hope. Spiritual health is not about

---

[59] Jennings, The God-Shaped Brain, 40.

[60] David A. Seamands, *Healing for Damaged Emotions* (Wheaton, IL: Victor, 1981), 52.

vague feelings or rituals; it is about living in relationship with the living God who created us and redeemed us through His Son.

Chapter Summary

We have discussed how our view of God, self, and others affects our mental, physical, social, and spiritual health. Viewing God as a benevolent, loving God alleviates stress circuits and puts the brain in a better position of being healthy, giving us freedom to think healthy thoughts. Viewing God as a loving God puts our physical body in a better position to function properly, leading to better health by changing our DNA for the better. Holding the right idea about who God is helps us interact socially in a healthier, more productive manner. We model the God we worship—worship a God of love and become more loving, worship an authoritarian god and become more abusive to others. Lastly, how we view God affects our spiritual health, for we can never experience healthy spirituality if we do not know the altruistic, loving God of the Bible.

Now that we know where our distorted view of God, self, and others originated, and what the damaging effects are, in the next chapter, we will discover what God reveals about Himself in the Bible, what is revealed about our new identity in Christ, and how to view others through the lens of God's love.

These consequences reveal just how deeply our beliefs affect every part of life. A distorted view of God does not remain hidden in the mind—it shapes health, relationships, and spiritual vitality. But God has not left us without hope. In the next chapter, we will turn to Scripture itself to see how God reveals His true nature, our new identity in Christ, and how this truth reshapes the way we love others.

Chapter Three Reflection & Discussion Guide

For personal journaling, small group dialogue, or ministry training

Personal Reflection

1. How has your view of God—whether loving or harsh—affected your mental or emotional health?
2. Can you think of a time when distorted self-beliefs influenced your choices or relationships?
3. In what ways have wrong ideas about God shaped your ability to extend grace to others?

Bible Engagement

1. Read **Matthew 6:25–34**. How does Jesus' teaching here confront anxiety and fear that come from a distorted view of God?
2. Reflect on **Philippians 4:6–8**. What do these verses teach about the renewing of our thoughts, and how does that connect to healthier living?
3. Read **Ephesians 4:17–24**. How does Paul describe the connection between wrong thinking, unhealthy living, and spiritual renewal?

Group Discussion

1. Where do you see the effects of distorted views of God most strongly today—mental struggles, physical issues, relational breakdowns, or spiritual drift?
2. How can believers come alongside one another in addressing the consequences of false beliefs about God?

3. What practices can help a community grow in holding a healthier, more biblical view of God, self, and others?

Want to go deeper?

Download the free companion journal at 180perspective.com/the-God-shaped-life-study for extended prompts, prayers, and space to reflect.

Chapter Four: What the Bible Reveals about God, Self, and Others

Introduction

"Show me what you think is at the heart of the universe and I will show you what will be at the heart of your conduct."[61]

What comes to your mind when you think of God? There are probably just as many answers to that question as there are people answering. According to Pew Research, 90 percent of Americans believe in some kind of higher power, though only 56 percent profess faith in the God of the Bible.[62] However, a Baylor University study found that 77 percent of Americans hold a distorted view of God, with the dominant image being that of an authoritarian deity.[63] This is a conundrum since 33.6 percent of those holding to a biblical view of God could be identified as Evangelical Protestants, yet only one in four of them believes the Bible defines God as benevolent.

"Far too many people have a surface knowledge of God. They know something about Him, but they do not know Him," explains Charles Stanley.[64]

---

[61] E. Stanley Jones, *The Christ of the Mount: A Working Philosophy of Life* (Nashville: Abingdon, 1931), 20.

[62] Pew Research Center, "America's Changing Religious Landscape," May 12, 2015, https://www.pewresearch.org

[63] Froese and Bader, *America's Four Gods*, 5.

[64] Stanley, The Wonderful Spirit-Filled Life, 29.

Indeed, there has been a plethora of books written about God in attempts to explain and reveal who He is. Some of those works are beneficial, while others are downright damaging. My attempt here is not to duplicate someone else's efforts. Rather, I want to give you a general introduction to what God has revealed about Himself. Think of this chapter as taking you to the shore of a great sea and getting your toes wet, in hopes that you will be excited enough to begin a deeper study of what God wants you to know about Himself. Hopefully, you will be so moved that you will plunge into the depths and experience for yourself the majesty and mysteries of God's loving character.

The God of Love

The best place to start is in the book of Hebrews, where we are told that, "God, after He spoke long ago to the fathers in the prophets in many portions and in many ways, in these last days has spoken to us in His Son" (Heb. 1:1–2). Notice that this Scripture describes that in former times God spoke, singularly "spoke." This indicates that the message was the same, even though that message was delivered through the prophets in many portions and in many ways. The Greek word translated as "portions" suggests that God spoke in multiple parts or on various occasions. In addition, God also spoke in various ways. Therefore, God spoke on many occasions and in multiple ways through the prophets to the fathers, but the message God conveyed was intended to reveal something that He wanted mankind to know —a singular message that revealed God's loving nature. John Walton writes,[65]

God has a plan in history that he is sovereignly executing. The goal of that plan is for him to be in a relationship with the people whom he has created. It would be difficult for people to enter into a relationship with a God whom they do not know. If his nature were concealed, obscured, or distorted, an honest relationship would be impossible. To clear the way for this relationship, God has undertaken, as a primary objective, a program of self-revelation. He wants people to know him. The mechanism that drives this program is the covenant, and the instrument is Israel. The purpose of the covenant is to reveal God.

And by God revealing himself, his loving nature would be exposed. When God passed by Moses and let Moses see the backside of his glory, God proclaimed, "The LORD, the LORD God, compassionate and gracious, slow to anger, and abounding in lovingkindness and truth" (Exod. 34:6). The Hebrew word for *proclaimed* is the word meaning "to call." In other words, God was calling out his attributes to Moses. Notice that every one of these attributes could be attributed to a loving act or a loving state of being, including the word for *truth*, which could also be translated as *faithfulness*. However, one of the attributes God calls out about Himself specifically signifies that He is abounding in lovingkindness.

Another example of God revealing Himself to Israel is when Moses led Israel to Mt. Sinai after the Egyptian

---

[65] John H. Walton, Old Testament Theology for Christians (2017), 43.

escape. Once they arrived at Mt. Sinai, the Lord's revelation of himself on the mountain top was too great for the Hebrews—as if all the great miraculous plagues on Egypt, the miraculous parting of the sea, the miraculous watering and feeding in the desert, the deliverances, and the pillars of fire and clouds were not enough—"All the people perceived the thunder and the lightning flashes and the sound of the trumpet and the mountain smoking; and when the people saw it, they trembled and stood at a distance" (Exod. 20:18). They were so afraid that they approached Moses saying, "Speak to us yourself and we will listen; but let not God speak to us, or we will die" (Exod. 20:19).

Moses replied saying, "Do not be afraid; for God is come in order to test you, in order that the fear of him may remain with you, so that you may not sin" (Exod. 20:20). The word *to test* in the Hebrew means to do something to bring about an end result—similar to training to be better at something. What Moses was implying is that the Lord was training them to understand who He is: His character, in order that they would pay attention to His instructions so that they would not sin. To sin meant going on a wrong path, to go astray, or to function outside of God's original design and purpose for them. Remember, God wanted to have a relationship with his creation. If Israel went astray, it would lose the opportunity to be in a relationship with Him.

What was God's response? God spoke again, but this time he instructed Moses to say to Israel, "You yourselves have seen that I have spoken to you from heaven. You shall not make other gods besides me; gods of silver or gods of gold, you shall not make for yourselves" (Exod. 20:22–23). In other words, God was instructing Israel that

70

since they had seen that He had spoken to them from heaven, they should recognize who He is and not make false gods of silver or gold. Why? Because God knew that if Israel worshiped false gods, it would muddle their relationship with Him so that they would not be able to comprehend who He really is.

Moses interceded for the Hebrews, wrote down all the details of the covenant, and recounted it to Israel. All Israel professed that they would follow the instructions. God then called Moses and the elders of Israel up to visit Him on the mountain. In response, "Moses went up with Aaron, Nadab and Abihu, and seventy of the elders of Israel, and they saw the God of Israel; and under his feet there appeared to be a pavement of sapphire clear as the sky itself" (Exod. 24:9–10).

Moses and the elders must have gone back down after the viewing of God because the narrative goes on to immediately disclose, "Now the Lord said to Moses, 'Come up to Me on the mountain and remain there, and I will give you the stone tablets with the law and the commandment which I have written for their instruction'" (Exod. 24:12). Moses spent a great deal of time on the mountain in God's presence while God taught him about the covenant, the tabernacle, and so forth. However, while Moses was gone, Israel grew impatient and decided to go against God's instruction, making for themselves a god of gold, a golden calf, and began to worship it.

This episode illustrates how quickly Israel departed from God's revealed truth. Even the seventy elders who had just received a special revelation of God did not stand against the people's idolatry. Despite all the ways

God had revealed Himself, they fell into the very sin God had warned them about: functioning outside His original design and intention. The result was judgment and broken fellowship.

The Sinai account demonstrates a central point: when God speaks, He reveals His loving character so that His people might know Him and live in relationship with Him. When that revelation is rejected out of fear or distorted through idolatry, the relationship breaks down. God's purpose in speaking through the prophets was always to reveal His character so that His people would not worship false gods. If Israel had truly embraced God for who He revealed Himself to be, they would have remained in right relationship with Him and been a witness to the nations.

Jesus Christ was not another prophet of God, as some claim, but was God incarnate. The writer of Hebrews clarifies who the Son is: "Whom He appointed heir of all things, through whom He also made the world" (Heb. 1:2). A few verses later we are told that the Son "is the radiance of His [God's] glory and the exact representation of [God's] nature" (Heb. 1:3). F. F. Bruce suggests, "He is the reflection of God's glory."[66] Donald Guthrie adds, "The word translated 'radiance' (*apaugasma*), used only here in the New Testament, carries the sense of 'splendor' or 'intense brightness.' So as the 'radiance of his glory,' the Son is the manifestation of the person and presence of God."[67]

---

[66] F. F. Bruce, *The Epistle to the Hebrews*, rev. ed. (1990), 50.

[67] Donald Guthrie, *The Letter to the Hebrews* (1983), 67.

The writer of Hebrews was not satisfied with just stating that Jesus is the brilliant manifestation of the presence of God, but he also declared that Jesus is the exact representation of God's nature or character. The word *nature* is translated from the Greek *hypostasis*, meaning "the essential or basic structure/nature of an entity, substantial nature, essence, actual being, reality." In other words, Jesus is the exact actual being—the reality—of God and represents everything God chose to reveal about His character through Him.

What has Jesus revealed about God's character? While answering this exhaustively would go beyond the scope of our introduction, we can point to one profound aspect of God's loving nature: His act of love in laying down His life.

It is written in John 3:16, "For God so loved the world, that He gave His only begotten Son, that whoever believes in Him shall not perish, but have eternal life." Even though this verse tells us that God, motivated by love, gave His Son (Jesus), the Son was working in accord with God's love and freely giving of Himself, also motivated by love. When speaking about His imminent crucifixion, Jesus said, "No one has taken it away from Me, but I lay it down on My own initiative. I have authority to lay it down, and I have authority to take it up again" (John 10:18). D. A. Carson states, "The climax of the Son's mission is itself grounded in the love of God."[68] This is confirmed in 1 John 3:16, where it is written, "We know love by this, that He laid down His life for us." In addition, Jesus said to His disciples, "Greater love has no

---

[68] D. A. Carson, *The Gospel According to John* (1991), 385.

one than this, that one lay down his life for his friends" (John 15:13).

Indeed, God has spoken in these last days through His Son Jesus Christ, and among other things, Jesus has made known the loving character of God through His life and death. Again, the goal here is not to give an exhaustive account of every way God spoke in both the Old and New Testaments, but to provide a general introduction to whet your appetite and start you on a path of investing in knowing God's loving character.

If God has revealed Himself as love through His Son, then it follows that those who belong to Christ must understand themselves through that same lens of love. To see God rightly is to begin seeing ourselves rightly—as new creations in Christ.

A New Creation in Christ

"As individuals, we will consistently act according to the way we see ourselves."[69]

One of the greatest challenges just about all of us face is a healthy self-image. There are numerous reasons we develop poor self-images, but the most prominent reason, as Ziglar points out, is the fact that "We live in a negative society and deal constantly with negative individuals."[70] The problem with living in a negative society is that we tend to allow how others make us feel about ourselves to determine our self-image and self-worth. It is like one of those mirrors at a fun house—or a horror house to

---

[69] Ziglar, See You at the Top, 65.

[70] Ziglar, See You at the Top, 66.

some—where the mirror projects back a distorted image of reality. If we believe the distorted projection, then we accept that image as reality. For example, if Johnny is consistently told by his family that he is stupid, then Johnny is going to grow up thinking he is stupid, even if he is not. And if Johnny sees himself as stupid, then he is going to behave like he's stupid.

This is why distorted self-perceptions matter so deeply. When we fail to see our true identity in Christ, we often fall back into false labels that shape how we live. One small but telling example illustrates this point. I remember seeing a bumper sticker some time ago that said, "Sinner saved by grace!" Now, if the person who placed that bumper sticker on the vehicle really saw themselves as a sinner saved by grace, then how is that person going to live? As a sinner saved by grace! I would venture to guess that person is struggling with temptation and experiences victory very seldom. A person like that is stuck in a repetitive cycle of sin, repentance, sin again, and clings to the belief that they will not fully experience freedom from sin until entry into heaven.

The only hope for a person who sees themselves like this is the Scripture: "If we confess our sins, He is faithful and righteous to forgive us our sins and to cleanse us from all unrighteousness" (1 Jn. 1:9). However, they forget that a few verses earlier it says, "If we say that we have fellowship with Him and yet walk in the darkness, we lie and do not practice the truth" (1 Jn. 1:6). The next verse reveals that, "If we walk in the Light as He Himself is in the Light, we have fellowship with one another, and the blood of Jesus His Son cleanses us from all sin" (1 Jn. 1:7). You cannot walk in the Light and practice sin at the same time; sin is the result of walking in darkness, and walking in darkness distorts your self-image and self-worth. Thank God that He has provided a way out of the darkness!

However, as we will see shortly, a true believer in Christ is no longer a sinner saved by grace but rather a past sinner who, through God's grace, has been recreated to be the righteousness of God in Christ.

In the following, I am going to give you a brief introduction to what the Bible says about your identity as a believer in Christ. My hope is that it will prompt you to begin investing in discovering your new identity in Christ and, in turn, begin to live a life more in line with the reality of who you are as a new creation in Christ. In other words, raise the ceiling of living in line with who God created you to be. If you want victory over sin, you have to change your self-image from a sinner to a saint. You will not live like a saint if you do not see yourself as a saint.

The apostle Paul tells us that, "If any man is in Christ, he is a new creature; the old things passed away; behold, new things have come" (2 Cor. 5:17, NASB).

Ephesians chapter one begins by informing us that we have been blessed, "with every spiritual blessing in the heavenly places in Christ" (Eph. 1:3). I believe the rest of Ephesians was written to reveal to us what our blessed new identity in Christ looks like and how to keep away from things that damage that new identity. For example, Ephesians prompts us to abstain from participating with those who walk "according to the course of this world" (Eph. 2:2). I believe the reason for that is that walking as the world walks destroys our self-identity and self-worth, not to mention that it destroys our perception of God as well.

Paul instructs us: "Let us keep living by that same standard to which we have attained. Brethren, join in following my example, and observe those who walk according to the pattern you have in us. For many walk, of whom I often told you, and now tell you even weeping, that they are enemies of the cross of Christ, whose end is destruction, whose god is their appetite, and whose glory is in their shame, who set their minds on earthly things" (Phil. 3:16–19, NASB).

In an earlier verse Paul revealed the key to his exemplary lifestyle: "I count all things to be loss in view of the surpassing value of knowing Christ Jesus my Lord, for whom I have suffered the loss of all things, and count them but rubbish so that I may gain Christ, and may be found in Him, not having a righteousness of my own derived from the Law, but that which is through faith in Christ, the righteousness which comes from God on the basis of faith" (Phil. 3:8–9, NASB). Notice the contrast in these verses. Paul encourages us to live according to the same lifestyle he and his comrades in the faith are living, which is the exact opposite of those who walk according to the flesh. For if you walk according to the flesh, you will carry out the deeds of the flesh.

Paul goes on to clarify our past condition with our new identity in Christ:

You were dead in your trespasses and sins, in which you formerly walked according to the course of this world, according to the prince of the power of the air, of the spirit that is now working in the sons of disobedience. Among them, we too all formerly lived in the lusts of our flesh, indulging the desires of the flesh and of the

*mind, and were by nature children of wrath, even as the rest. But
God, being rich in mercy, because of His great love with which He
loved us, even when we were dead in our transgressions, made us
alive together with Christ (by grace you have been saved), and raised
us up with Him, and seated us with Him in the heavenly places in
Christ Jesus, so that in the ages to come He might show the
surpassing riches of His grace in kindness toward us in Christ
Jesus. For by grace you have been saved through faith; and that not
of yourselves, it is the gift of God; not as a result of works, so that
no one may boast, for we are His workmanship, created in Christ
Jesus for good works, which God prepared beforehand so that we
would walk in them.* (Eph. 2:1–10, NASB)

Notice the comparison in these verses. We were once
dead in our living outside of God's original design and
purpose. In other words, we lived life as reflected to us by
the world and the satanic power behind its ways, which
fed us distorted self-images. Yet while we were in that
state of distorted self-perception, God went to work and
refashioned us, raising us up with Christ into a new life so
that we would walk according to God's design and
purpose. Now, as Paul so eloquently stated, we are to
consider that "in reference to your former manner of
life," we "lay aside the old self, which is being corrupted
in accordance with the lusts of deceit, and that," we "be
renewed in the spirit of" our "mind, and put on the new
self, which in the likeness of God has been created in
righteousness and holiness of the truth" (Eph. 4:22–24).

In Colossians 1:21–22 Paul further informs us that,
"Although you were formerly alienated and hostile in
mind, engaged in evil deeds, yet He has now reconciled
you in His fleshly body through death, in order to present
you before Him holy and blameless and beyond
reproach." And a few verses earlier, Paul states that we

78

should joyously give, "Thanks to the Father, who has qualified us to share in the inheritance of the saints in Light. For He rescued us from the domain of darkness, and transferred us to the kingdom of His beloved Son, in whom we have redemption, the forgiveness of sins" (Col. 1:11–14).

Again, these are just a few verses that reveal to us what God has said about our new identity in Christ. If we start believing God's declaration about our new identity as a saint in Christ, then we are going to be in a better position to live out the truth of who we really are. So, the next time you struggle with your self-identity and self-worth, grab hold of the Bible and allow its reflection of you to set your mind straight.

And if our identity has been reshaped in Christ, then that identity must naturally affect how we view and treat others.

Loving Others

"The way you see people is the way you treat them, and the way you treat them is what they become."[71]

One of the greatest distortions affecting us as individuals, and which brings an unnecessary amount of harm to the table, is our perception of others. How we view others determines how we treat them. For example, if I perceive you as an untrustworthy person, then I will treat you accordingly. On the other hand, if I see you as a saint, then I will treat you as one. If one social group views another in a negative light, they are likely to treat

---

[71] Johann Wolfgang von Goethe, quoted in Emil Ludwig, *Goethe: The History of a Man* (1928), 312.

the other group in a similarly unfavorable manner. If one ethnic group sees another ethnic group as not equal, then that ethnic group is going to treat the other ethnic group badly. If a man sees a woman as an object, then he is going to treat the woman as an object and not as a person. If a woman views a man as a means, then she will treat that man as a means and not as a person. We can often see these distortions played out in relationships.

From a domestic perspective, relationships can be one of the most difficult situations we find ourselves in. On the other hand, relationships can be one of the greatest blessings we have on this planet. A large part of determining whether a relationship is a curse or a blessing has to do with either our perception of the other person or the other person's perception of us. Our perception of others often lays the groundwork for whether we desire to enter some sort of relationship at whatever level. Often, we enter into relationships because we somehow perceive that the person we are seeking to enter the relationship with has something to bring to the relationship—something we desire or long for. Usually, the desire is to feel a sense of unconditional love and encouragement, but often it is the desire to get something from the other person rather than to give.

We are often drawn to people who make us feel a sense of being needed or cared about, even if, and often in abusive situations, the sense of feeling needed or loved is a distortion of reality. By distortion, I mean that some people's perception of being loved or needed is so skewed that even the acts of the person abusing them are perceived as love, when in reality the abusive person is using them for their own gratification or gain (as an object or a means rather than a person with hopes and dreams).

Therefore, relationships can be complex if you take into consideration the fact that we enter relationships with expectations and desires, hoping the other party involved will participate. However, quite often we forget that the other person entered the relationship with their own expectations and desires as well, and sometimes what they wanted out of the relationship is quite the opposite of what we wanted. This can lead to escalated emotional situations and often end in the destruction of the relationship. In some instances, the emotional escalation stemming from disappointment can lead to extremes where one or both parties develop a desire to physically harm or mentally abuse the other person.

We have all heard the statistics that over half of marriages end in divorce, and Christians are not immune. Why? Relational problems are the culprit, whether the relational discrepancy arises from one or both of those involved. If we could get past our selfish desire to "get" something from the relationship and instead give something to the relationship, we would be in a much better position for a healthier relationship. I am not suggesting that we become a doormat for someone's selfishness. What I am suggesting is that if we approach the relationship with the intent of bringing a sincere interest in the well-being of the other person, the relationship would blossom, at least in most situations.

The best way to change how we approach relationships is to change our motives and desires. With that said, let us look at what the Bible says about how we should view others. Again, this is going to be a brief introduction into how to view others through the lens of God's love.

In the Bible, love is the identifying characteristic of believers in Christ. The apostle John writes, "Beloved, if God so loved us, we also ought to love one another . . . if we love one another, God abides in us, and His love is perfected in us" (1 John 4:11–12). As well, Paul exhorts believers to "build up the body of Christ in love" (Eph. 4:15–16). And Jesus gave this all-important announcement to his disciples, "By this all men will know that you are My disciples, if you have love for one another" (John 13:35). Believers are also challenged to, "Therefore be imitators of God, as beloved children; and walk in love" (Eph. 5:1–2). Love is the kingdom in which the believer resides.

In the Bible, there are several Greek words translated as "love." However, in each of the instances listed above that describe the characteristics of God, Jesus, or the believer in Christ, the Greek word *agapē* is used and defined as "the quality of warm regard for and interest in another."[72] In other words, to be genuinely interested in the well-being of another without desiring or expecting anything in return. To be genuinely interested in the well-being of another, you must be willing to give something of yourself to them. More specifically, you must give of your time, your thoughts, and occasionally material possessions with the sincerest desire to help the person be better, stronger, or some other benefit that makes them a healthier person, without expecting anything in

---

[72] Walter Bauer, Frederick William Danker, William F. Arndt, and F. Wilbur Gingrich, *A Greek-English Lexicon of the New Testament and Other Early Christian Literature*, 3rd ed. (2000), 7.

return. The way the Bible describes this kind of love is giving that goes before your own desires or wants.

However, the modern idea of love involves an intense feeling or deep affection. Though intense feelings and deep affections appear to be self-focused, most people will only commit to love if they sense that there is some benefit in it for them. In other words, most people think like this (though probably not consciously): "I am willing to maintain intense feelings for you if you continue to hand over what drew me to the relationship in the first place, and at the same level I received at the beginning of the relationship."

These distorted expectations of love are not just theoretical; they play out in real relationships. One counseling session I recall captures this dynamic clearly. Take, for example, Jim and Sally. They both sat in my office seeking a solution to their marriage problems. They felt that they were at a point where they were going to call it quits. They came to see me as a last-ditch effort to save their marriage. When I asked Jim to reminisce about why he married Sally, he began to recount how he thought Sally was going to be this for him or do that for him. Sally's response was similar. It appeared that both were approaching the relationship from an "I want, and you give" mentality. It did not take long before neither one was able to perform at the capacity the other wanted, so problems began. Jim's biggest pet peeve was that he wanted Sally to cook, keep the house clean, and be there to cuddle with him every night. If Sally was able to perform to the capacity of Jim's expectations, he maintained his intense feelings for Sally. Sally wanted Jim to take care of her and make her feel like she was special.

However, Jim's income was not enough for the house and the two cars they were financing, so Sally had to take on a job. After work, when Sally arrived home, she was too tired to cook and clean the house, and snuggling was out of the question. Jim was disappointed in Sally's lack of living up to his expectations, which caused him to push away from her. Sally was beginning to feel a sense of rejection by Jim, which caused her to pull away as a form of protecting her feelings. The downward spiral continued until it almost snapped their marriage.

Things changed for Jim and Sally as we discovered what the Bible teaches about love. Jim began to look at Sally through a lens of looking out for her best interest without expecting anything in return, and Sally did the same toward Jim. Today, Jim and Sally are more in love— real love—than they were when they first decided to get married.

Now, to make things clear, this God-kind of love is not a license for others to take advantage of you. You do not give a drug addict money just because he says something like, "If you were a real Christian, you would help me!" Or a controlling person who says, "If you really loved me, you would . . .!" These are demands that are not always in the best interest of the one demanding. If you reject these kinds of demands, you are not being unloving. In fact, your denial of their requests could be very loving because you are looking out for their well-being. If you were to give in to their demands, it could cause further damage to their physical or mental well-being, or it could strengthen their selfish desires so that they think they are in control of you and want something more from you in the future.

No, real biblical love is an altruistic love. This is the kind of love that is genuinely interested in the well-being of others without expecting or wanting anything in return. This kind of love requires that you deny your own selfish desires and wants. This is in accord with Jesus' statement: "If anyone wishes to come after Me, he must deny himself, and take up his cross and follow Me" (Mark 8:34). Following Jesus meant death to personal and selfish interests, which, prior to being a new creation, was the outward expression of an inward heart condition—one of functioning outside the design laws of God and traditionally understood to be the sinful nature. However, as new creations in Christ, believers are now to "imitate God and walk" in warm regard and sincere interest for others—placing others' interests above their own (Eph. 5:1–2). In contrast, Paul describes what walking as the nations who do not walk in love do in Eph. 4:17–19: "So this I say, and affirm together with the Lord, that you walk no longer just as the Gentiles also walk, in the futility of their mind, being darkened in their understanding, excluded from the life of God because of the ignorance that is in them, because of the hardness of their heart; and they, having become callous, have given themselves over to sensuality for the practice of every kind of impurity with greediness."

So then, believers are to be identified for their warm regard for and sincere interest in others. Their love seeks to build others up and help them find completeness in Christ (1 Cor. 1:10; 2 Cor. 13:9, 11; Col. 1:28; 2:10; 1 Thes. 5:23; James 1:4; and 1 John 1:4). It is by this kind of love that the world will know who the followers of Christ are.

Chapter Summary

In this chapter, we have seen that God has revealed Himself as a God of love, both in the Old and New Testaments. We have also discovered that in Christ, believers are given a new identity as saints rather than sinners, called to walk in the light of His righteousness. Finally, we considered how this identity is meant to reshape our relationships, calling us to love others with the same *agapē* love that God has shown us.

In the next chapter, you will learn practical ways to continue on the path of discovering the God-shaped life by renewing your mind in Christ. As your mind is renewed, you will see God for who He really is, embrace your new creation identity more fully, and learn how to walk in genuine love toward others.

God has shown Himself as a God of love, has given us a new identity in Christ, and calls us to reflect that love in how we treat others. These truths set the foundation for transformation. In the next chapter, we will take practical steps for living out this God-shaped life— renewing our minds, deepening prayer, engaging Scripture, and sharing our faith with others.

Chapter Four Reflection & Discussion Guide

For personal journaling, small group dialogue, or ministry training

Personal Reflection

1. How does seeing God as love challenge or affirm the way you've thought about Him in the past?
2. When you think of yourself as a new creation in Christ, what changes most in the way you see yourself?
3. Who in your life is God calling you to love in a deeper, more Christlike way?

Bible Engagement

1. Read **1 John 4:7–12**. What does this passage reveal about the nature of God's love and how it should be expressed in us?
2. Reflect on **2 Corinthians 5:17**. How does Paul describe what it means to be made new in Christ?
3. Read **John 13:34–35**. According to Jesus, how should love be the defining mark of His followers?

Group Discussion

1. How does a right view of God as love reshape the way we live together as believers?
2. What practical ways can the church demonstrate what it means to be a community of people "made new" in Christ?
3. How does living out God's kind of love stand out in today's culture, and why is it such powerful evidence of the gospel?

Want to go deeper?

Download the free companion journal at 180perspective.com/the-God-shaped-life-study for extended prompts, prayers, and space to reflect.

Let me know when you're ready to move on to Chapter Five or if you'd like help styling these guides into your manuscript layout. You're building something truly life-giving here.

Chapter Five: Practical Steps to Discover the Life God Intended

If you have stuck with me this far, then you must be ready to begin the journey to discovering the God-shaped life. You want to know what to do to see God for who He really is. You want to change your self-image to be more in line with who God recreated you to be in Christ. You want to learn to love others with God's kind of love. You want to take off the old and put on the new. Then let us get started!

In this chapter, I will offer some practical steps you can take to see God for who He really is, change your self-identity to saint, and learn to love others altruistically. We will begin by learning to control our cognitive gaze—in other words, control what we put into our minds. Then, we will discover how to pray in faith for wisdom and understanding. We especially need wisdom and knowledge when reading the Word of God. Once we have learned to pray in faith, I will show a simple approach to reading the Bible. Afterwards, I will help you learn to meditate on God's Word in a simple but profound way. Lastly, I will show you how to share what you have learned from this book with others in a simple but effective manner.

Control Cognitive Gaze

At the beginning of this book, I shared with you the statistics that most Christians have a distorted view of God, resulting in a moral dilemma where Christians are no different in their actions than the secular world. I helped you to see that the reason we got into this dilemma is because of what has gone into our minds. The

89

truth is that who we are and what we believe is the product of other people's contributed ideas into our minds. Now is the time to take control of what goes into your mind.

The Bible tells us to "take every thought captive." Why? Because if we allow our thoughts to run wild, we are setting the precedent for the performances or life activities that we believe will get us to the destination we are working towards; if our thoughts are all over the place, then the destination is all over the place. Such a life is unstable with no set destination; such has been my former life.

The truth is, if we look closer at 2 Corinthians 10:3–5, we discover that the enemy seeks to destroy our thoughts and beliefs, erecting fortresses around them to prevent us from experiencing God for who He truly is. This, in turn, destroys our hope. Without hope, life is meaningless.

In Paul's second letter to the Corinthian church, he stated that on his next visit, "I propose to be courageous against some, who regard us as if we walked according to the flesh" (2 Cor. 10:2). Apparently, there were some in the church at Corinth who accused the Apostle Paul and Timothy and their companions of being fleshly in their deeds. Paul responded, "Though we walk in the flesh, we do not war according to the flesh" (2 Cor. 10:3).

Paul then proceeds to define what the war is and how it is fought. "For the weapons of our warfare are not of the flesh, but divinely powerful for the destruction of fortresses. We are destroying speculations and every lofty thing raised against the knowledge of God, and we are taking every thought captive to the obedience of Christ" (2 Cor. 10:4–5).

Let us break these verses down. The word warfare comes from a Greek word meaning campaign, which gives the impression that in the war Paul is referring to, he and his comrades have an organized offensive to achieve a goal. I find this interesting because Paul and his friends' methods and authority were being questioned. We know this because Paul said that some regard "us (again, a reference to Paul and his companions), as if we walked in the flesh." Such an accusation would have put many of us on the defensive. However, Paul was not defensive in his reply; instead, he revealed a little something about his campaign objective, which included destroying the fortress of pessimistic thinking of those who would accuse him and his coworkers of being fleshly—notice that it is the distorted thinking that Paul is addressing and not the physical person(s) who are making the accusation.

The weapons used in Paul's organized offensive are "not of the flesh, but divinely powerful." The description of the type of weaponry Paul is using reveals that the war is being waged in the theater of the mind (remember that earlier in the book, we discussed the mind not being physical). In addition, the fact that the weaponry is divinely powerful exposes the truth that it is the very power of God.

Next, Paul discloses the campaign objective: "the destruction of fortresses." In Greek, the term "fortress" referred to a strong military fortification, and within the context of this passage, the fortresses are those that the enemy has set up. The Greek word for "destruction" meant to dismantle or take down and render obsolete. In other words, a fortress was erected to protect the people (including those who were taken as captives) and the things behind the walls of the fortress. If the fortress is taken down, the people and the items that the fortress is meant to protect would be exposed and subject to being taken captive.

Paul then digs a little deeper and reveals what the fortresses are: "We are destroying speculations and every lofty thing raised against the knowledge of God" (2 Cor. 10:5). The word destroying is the same word used in v. four and has the same meaning; the dismantling of something, and in this case, Paul is telling us that he is dismantling the enemy fortress of speculation. Speculation comes from a Greek word that is the product of the thoughts that preoccupy your mind. In other words, speculation is the product of taking incoming information and allowing that information to preoccupy your thoughts until you make a calculated judgment. Calculated judgments align with one's beliefs. If you make a judgment about something, then you have formulated a belief about it.

Again, since Paul is discussing the enemy fortress of speculation, we can assume that the enemy has managed to supply wrong and fleshly information, which has entered the minds of some of the people involved in the Corinthian church. These infected individuals have taken the falsified information and given thought to it, made calculated decisions or wrong conclusions, and have adopted distorted belief systems as a result. The enemy has now established formidable military fortresses in the minds of these infected individuals.

However, it does not end there, because another fortress—a high and lofty one—has been raised in some of their minds, which prevents them from knowing and experiencing God. The Greek word for high and lofty comes from an astronomical term indicating a linear extension that stretches into the heavenly realm. However, some theologians think it has something to do with arrogance. I believe both are true of the situation. So then, here we have an erected stronghold of the enemy that causes arrogance in the infected, as well as a fortress that extends into God's heavenly realm, which prevents those infected from experientially knowing God. The implication of this is that the enemy can even reach into the minds of those who have been adopted into God's kingdom. This means that Christians are not impervious to having fortresses erected in their minds which hinder their comprehension of God's great love and rob them of experiencing His divine power in their lives—this is why most Christians are no different morally than the secular world.

Those who are captive and infected with the enemy's military strongholds of distorted beliefs and are deprived of being able to experientially know God are prisoners of someone else's ideals. These ideals originated with wrong information and a lack of wisdom to discern the truth. The enemy knew this and exploited the situation, launching a campaign of his own with the calculated agenda of taking control of their mind and keeping them from experiencing and knowing God's great love for them. The Apostle Peter warned, "Your adversary, the devil, prowls around like a roaring lion, seeking someone to devour" (1 Pet. 5:8). The enemy has his special forces working overtime to take control of our thoughts and beliefs.

Paul understood this war better than most, and because of some special revelations, he was made aware of the divinely powerful weapons (the Word of God). Paul had been thoroughly trained on how to effectively and efficiently use the weapon to dismantle and render useless the enemy's military strongholds in the minds of the captive. In the last half of v. 5, Paul states that he and his team are "taking every thought captive to the obedience of Christ." That statement is Paul and his squad's objective for the offensive campaign with which they were engaged. And what was in the balance? What was going to happen if Paul's objective was not achieved? A few verses later, Paul stated, "But I am afraid that, as the serpent deceived Eve by his craftiness, your minds will be led astray from the simplicity and purity of devotion to Christ" (2 Cor. 11:3).

What does it mean to take every thought captive to the obedience of Christ? The Greek word for thought has the notion of a product of the intellectual processes of the mind. Obviously, this is a direct reference to the fortresses of the enemy. In addition, the concept of captive comes from a military word meaning to take prisoners of war, and in the context of this passage, it refers to the realized agenda of gaining control of. Next, the Greek word for obedience means a favorable hearing, which suggests being in line with the will of God or God's original purpose and design. What can we take from this? Paul is saying that he is dismantling and rendering obsolete the strongholds the enemy has over the Corinthian church's members and thereby setting free the captives so that they can live within God's original purpose and design. Ephesians 4:8 tells us that when Jesus ascended on high, He led captive a host of captives. In other words, Jesus took captive those who were captives of the enemy.

The good news is that God has used Paul's military campaign as a training tool to help us know how to use the divinely powerful Word of God to facilitate the destruction of the enemy's strongholds and fortresses. Once the enemy's fortresses have been dismantled and rendered obsolete, our intellectual capacities and belief systems will be set free, clearing the way to see God for who He really is. Knowing God as a benevolent, loving God will keep our beliefs and thoughts in line with God's original purpose and design. Praise God!

But how do we do this? First, we must control our cognitive gaze. In other words, we must control what we allow into our minds and what we allow our minds to think about. Next time you get ready to watch the news media, a TV sitcom, a movie, view a website, or read a novel, ask yourself, "Will this plant negative and dark thoughts into my mind that will give the enemy permission to set up strongholds?" Remember, the enemy is waiting for an opportunity, for any chance to plant fortresses in your mind with the goal of keeping you from experiencing God for who He really is, destroying your self-image, and hindering social interaction.

Taking every thought captive requires that we take the thought and run it through a test grid to see if it is valid. For example, consider Mary's experience.

Mary called me one afternoon and, with a panicked voice, proceeded to tell me that her boyfriend (Dan) did something that gave her the impression that he might be seeing somebody else. I asked her to elaborate. After a series of explaining how it made her feel, she finally unveiled what happened. Apparently, after several wonderful days of spending quality time together, Dan made a statement that he needed a couple of days to deal with something personal. Mary was dumbfounded. She thought her and Dan's relationship was budding. She took Dan's announcement as a direct rejection. Mary's mind went wild with thoughts that turned into beliefs—beliefs that Dan was rejecting her and seeing someone else.

I explained to Mary that she was speculating and did not know anything beyond Dan's statement. Any thought involving filling in the blanks beyond what Dan said would be purely speculative. Mary's thoughts had run away with her, and because of failed relationships in the past, she assumed Dan was also going to abandon her, and her speculative thinking led her down a path of fear and hurt through which she developed a belief that Dan was seeing someone else. The enemy was setting up a stronghold that could have destroyed the relationship and physically caused damage to Mary's brain and physical health, not to mention future social interactions.

I suggested to Mary that she take her thoughts captive and text Dan and just simply state that she cares about him and is there for him if he needs anything. Dan responded and disclosed that he was dealing with a family situation involving his daughter, her abusive husband, and his grandchildren. Apparently, Dan was too embarrassed about the situation. Dan and Mary's relationship was in its early stages of development, and because of Dan's past experiences and preconceived ideas (largely speculative), he did not feel comfortable discussing his family problems with Mary. Mary's text opened the door for them to develop greater trust and is a lesson to both Dan and Mary about pulling down speculative strongholds and taking every thought captive.

Mary's situation is one form of a fortress that the enemy can set up in our minds. However, there are others. For example, in his book *The Propaganda Project*, Phil M. Williams writes, "We live in a society eerily similar to Aldous Huxley's *Brave New World*, where we're bombarded by entertainment and information to the point that we cannot decipher the truth from fiction, nor do we have much desire to do so."[73]

Why is this? I believe it has something to do with the fact that we were created with a natural propensity to believe what we are told, especially if we accept the one doing the telling as an authority figure. In addition, we have been so programmed to respond emotionally to entertainment media that if the one doing the telling causes us to respond emotionally, then we tend to accept their telling as fact.

The problem with this is that false ideas can be planted in our thoughts that develop into beliefs, which leave us captive to the enemy. The enemy then sets up fortresses around our beliefs to keep us captive. As captives behind enemy fortresses, our minds are prevented from seeing God for who He really is, seeing ourselves as the new creation in Christ that we are, and it distorts our ability to see others through the lens of God's love.

The aftermath is devastating to our lives, health, and social interactions.

You have probably seen this in some of the information passed off to us as factual in recent

---

[73] Phil M. Williams, *The Propaganda Project* (2017), 12.

situations. At the time of this writing, we are just exiting the first worldwide pandemic of our time, the COVID-19 scare. Our news media was all over the opportunity, inciting fear, which caused the ultimate shutdown of the world.

Any news that was in opposition to the "experts" was strategically removed from social media, and the major networks would not share any facts that were in opposition to their agenda. We were told that the virus jumped from a bat to humankind. However, that proved to be a mistruth.

We were also told that millions would die, yet that did not happen (it is unfortunate that any did die). People began to believe all this and responded by following orders to stay home. If you did venture out of your home for any reason, you must wear a mask and maintain six feet of distance. This prevention protocol was based on speculation since the "experts" kept saying that at the time, they did not know that much about the virus.

When the President of the United States found out about what social media was doing when selectively removing any information that was either politically biased or against the grain of the "experts," he signed an executive order to squelch their activities. Accusations began to arise that some of the major networks were producing "fake news." It turned out that the virus was only a major threat to people with compromised immune systems, which is true of any virus. It appears that more people die every year from the typical flu than from the COVID-19 virus (although there are conflicting reports about this; it depends on where you get your information).

Another situation that has arisen during this writing is the "Black Lives Matter" movement. You may recall how a black man was killed by a police officer. The media took the event and aroused a movement that caused protests and rioting. Even a section of Seattle was taken over by anarchists, and all police presence was eradicated.

I saw a video of a black lady freaking out and emotionally out of control; she kept expressing that because she was black, she could be shot by a police officer at any moment for no reason other than she is black. She was living in great fear. I also watched a video of a former black police officer who stated that the media had taken things way out of control. Apparently, according to the retired police officer, there are more white men who are killed by police every year than black people, and the prejudice the news media was inciting was unfounded.

Either way, the enemy has set up fortresses in the minds of the masses as people live in fear and hate. All this is caused by thoughts put into their minds that led to distorted belief systems. The fortresses the enemy has erected are causing people to respond in emotionally unhealthy ways. It is robbing them of being able to see God for who He really is—a benevolent God who loves them beyond their ability to comprehend. These enemy fortresses are holding captive the self-identity of untold thousands and maybe even millions, and robbing them of being able to socially interact in healthy ways.

My advice is to limit media influence, especially in the evening. You do not want to go to bed after being exposed to all the social unrest in our world, whether it is real or fabricated. I am not suggesting an ostrich-with-his-head-buried-in-the-sand approach, but that you be selective, limiting what and whom you get your information from. If you are able, do some fact-checking of your own. However, you need to be cautious if you fact-check, because much of what is passed off to us as "fact" is actually what is called "factoid," which is information that is passed off as evidence-based but really has no evidence supporting it, or if there is evidence offered it has been created by agenda-motivated individuals and typically turns out to be a twisting of truth. If you read or hear someone say "Experts say" or "According to (some authority)" but the expert or authority source is not revealed, then flag that message as possibly fictitious. As well, do not believe everything you hear; if your first response is "That's unbelievable!" then it could be false information meant to incite a line of thinking leading to a false belief whereby the enemy can set up fortresses in your mind.

Now more than ever, we need to pray and ask God for wisdom and understanding to navigate the dark waters of our turbulent times.

In summary, we have discussed that the first thing we need to do to know God for who He really is, see ourselves in the light of being a new creation in Christ, and learn to love others altruistically is to take control of our cognitive gaze. I shared with you what the Bible reveals about how the enemy tries to take our thoughts and subsequent beliefs captive and erect fortresses around them. I offered some limited but practical advice on how to destroy those fortresses by taking your thoughts captive and keeping them in line with God's original purpose and design. Next, I will help you learn to pray in faith.

Pray in Faith

In this segment, we are going to delve into what praying in faith for wisdom and understanding is all about. I am going to begin by going backwards; first, we will discuss what wisdom and understanding are, then what faith is, and lastly, we will tackle what prayer is.

The first part of my prayer life as a believer in Christ is no model for others to follow. My prayer life was more like the poster child for the life of a doubter. When I prayed, it was usually out of desperation, and my faith and hope in the answers were more like the foolish gambler spending his last dollar on a lottery ticket in hopes of winning a million, which really is not faith at all. It was not until years later, when I started investing attention (controlling my cognitive gaze), seeking wisdom and understanding, that I found a few verses which changed my perspective on how I could confidently and expectantly enter the Lord's presence in prayer with faith.

Where to focus our cognitive gaze that produces the greatest return on investment is the real question. There is no lack of attention-getters out there today. However, there is one place where you can focus your attention that has been producing unprecedented results for several thousand years, and that is through seeking wisdom and understanding. In other words, to find the God-shaped life, focus your cognitive gaze on the pursuit of wisdom and understanding. This may sound like a bold statement at this point, but I hope by the time you have finished reading this, I will have at least piqued your interest enough for you to want to know more about investing your attention in the pursuit of wisdom and understanding, and how those who find them are complete in life.

Several years ago, I was reading Proverbs and came across a couple of verses that caused me to pause and reflect: "How blessed is the man who finds wisdom, and the man who gains understanding, for her profit is better than the profit of silver, and her gain better than fine gold. She is more precious than jewels, and nothing you desire compares with her" (Prov. 3:13-15). As I read and pondered those verses, it dawned on me that I had spent most of my life valuing everything but wisdom and understanding.

As I continued to read Proverbs, I came across verse 18:1, which says, "He who separates himself seeks his own desire, He quarrels against all sound wisdom." The conviction was profound; I had spent a lifetime pursuing the values of my own desires, which were against sound wisdom. At that instant, I had a mighty "light bulb" moment of understanding.

Like most people, my life ambition had been to find happiness and fulfillment in the sense of realizing significance. The problem is that my ambitions were driven by the desires of the flesh. The flesh cares nothing about wisdom and understanding. When I came across Proverbs 3:13-15 and 18:1, I realized that wisdom and understanding were not just "a way," they were "the way" to finding the fulfillment of my desires.

Let us take a closer look at what wisdom and understanding are. Wisdom is the ability to make the right decisions based on knowledge, while understanding goes a little deeper. Understanding is the ability to perceive the meaning or significance of something. In other words, understanding is the ability to grasp the nature of something through experience.

Think about it like this: let's say a young boy named Ashton has been warned by his parents to stay away from the hot stove. His parents told him it would burn him. Ashton has the knowledge that the stove is hot and that it will burn him. However, Ashton does not yet have the understanding of what hot is until he touches the stove and burns himself. From then on, whenever Ashton hears the word hot, he understands the meaning through his experience. So, wisdom is the ability to use knowledge correctly, while understanding is the ability to grasp the significance of that knowledge through experience.

Now, let us transition to what the Bible has to say about wisdom and understanding. Proverbs 4:7 tells us, "The beginning of wisdom is: Acquire wisdom; And with all your acquiring, get understanding." This verse emphasizes that both wisdom and understanding are essential to living a fulfilled life. Proverbs 16:16 also tells us, "How much better it is to get wisdom than gold! And to get understanding is to be chosen above silver." Clearly, the Word of God places high value on wisdom and understanding.

It is also important to know what faith is. Hebrews 11:1 states, "Now faith is the assurance of things hoped for, the conviction of things not seen." Faith is not wishful thinking; it is the confident assurance that what God has promised will happen, even if we cannot see it with our physical eyes. Romans 10:17 also tells us, "So faith comes from hearing, and hearing by the word of Christ." Faith is birthed and sustained by the Word of God.

Now, how does prayer fit into all of this? Prayer is simply communication with God. It is not a ritual of reciting the same words over and over again, but it is a heartfelt conversation with the Creator of the universe. Prayer can be spoken or silent, formal or informal, but what is most important is that it is sincere and full of faith.

When we pray in faith for wisdom and understanding, we are asking God to reveal His truth to us in a way that we can grasp and apply to our lives. James 1:5 assures us of this: "But if any of you lacks wisdom, let him ask of God, who gives to all generously and without reproach, and it will be given to him." This is a promise we can stand on with confidence.

Therefore, praying in faith for wisdom and understanding means that we trust God to provide what we need to live in accordance with His purpose and design. It means that we are not relying on our own knowledge or abilities, but on God's divine insight and guidance. When we pray this way, we are positioning ourselves to live out the God-shaped life He created us for.

Building on the foundation of prayerful seeking for wisdom and understanding, the next vital step in our spiritual journey is learning how to read the Bible effectively. Engaging with Scripture not only deepens our relationship with God but also enhances our ability to discern His will and guidance in our lives. By approaching the Bible with an open heart and a desire to understand, we can draw on its timeless truths and teachings.

In the next section, we will explore practical approaches to reading the Bible that can enrich our spiritual lives and provide clearer insights into God's purpose for us.

How to Read the Bible

The Bible can be a bit daunting for some. I remember as a kid, around nine or ten years old, my family and I were staying in a motel. I was bored, so I picked up a King James version of the Bible left by the Gideons. I had never read the Bible before, nor did I know anything about it, other than somewhere I picked up the idea that it was a holy book. I tried to read from the beginning, Genesis chapter one, verse one. The first thing that struck me was the wording. I was intrigued by the opening story of creation, but when I began to read about God talking to man, I was lost with the thees and the thous. It was a foreign language and hard for my young mind to understand. I read for a few minutes and then put it down, never to pick it up again until years later.

For all those years of not reading the Bible, I still considered it a holy book and had also come to the understanding somewhere along the line that it was a book of "do this" and "do not do that," and then you can go to heaven. Finally, just prior to surrendering my life to Christ, a Bible had been given to me. Because I considered it a holy book, I would sleep with it under my pillow in hopes it would work like a magic charm and give me peace. Obviously, my perception of the Bible was distorted. I remember one early morning, I came home after partying all night. I was loaded with drugs and alcohol. I tried to read the Bible I had hidden under my pillow. Randomly, I opened it to somewhere in the middle and began to read. After a few sentences, I threw it against the wall and yelled, "Who wrote this garbage!?"

I do not remember what I read, but I do remember that it made no sense at all. I am sure it had something to do with my state of mind at the time.

I recall on another occasion seeing a stack of books placed on top of a Bible at someone's house. A man named Bill was visiting the owner of the house with me. Bill began to reprimand the Bible's owner about how the Bible is holy and nothing should be placed on it. Bill viewed the physical book as if it were holy and needed to be treated as such. What was interesting was that Bill never opened his Bible that I was aware of, and his life did not reflect a reverence for the Bible outside of holding it in high esteem.

Years later, I heard a debate between a couple of people about the actual physical book of the Bible. One person argued that it is nothing more than a leather-bound conglomerate of paper and ink and meant nothing more than that—unless it is opened, and the message is perceived. According to this person, it was the words that were holy and not the physical material. This person's argument was that the physical material—paper and ink, etc.—was not holier than any other language. Language, paper, and ink are just mediums, but the message is constant and never changing; the message is holy.

What is the Bible? The Bible is the Word of God. It is a library of sixty-six books written by about forty authors over a period of about 1,500 years. It is divided into two testaments, the Old and the New. The Old Testament contains thirty-nine books, and the New Testament contains twenty-seven books. The Old Testament was primarily written in Hebrew with a few passages in

Aramaic. The New Testament was written in Greek. Today, the Bible is translated into hundreds of languages.

The Bible is God's written revelation of Himself to humankind. It is a love story between God and humanity. It tells us who God is, who we are, what went wrong, and how God made it right through Jesus Christ. It is a story of redemption, restoration, and reconciliation. The Bible is not just a book of rules, although it contains commands. It is not just a book of history, although it contains historical accounts. It is not just a book of poetry, although it contains beautiful poetry. It is God's message of love, grace, and truth.

When we approach the Bible, we must do so with humility and openness. We must come with a heart that is willing to be taught, corrected, and transformed. The Bible is not meant to be used as a tool to prove ourselves right or to win arguments. It is meant to be a mirror to show us who we are and to point us to who God wants us to be. James 1:23-24 says, "For if anyone is a hearer of the word and not a doer, he is like a man who looks at his natural face in a mirror; for once he has looked at himself and gone away, he has immediately forgotten what kind of person he was."

To read the Bible effectively, it is helpful to ask three basic questions:

1. What does it say?
2. What does it mean?
3. How does it apply to my life?

"What does it say?" is the observation stage. Here we are simply looking at the text to see what it says. We are not interpreting or applying at this point, just observing.

"What does it mean?" is the interpretation stage. Here we are trying to understand what the text meant to the original audience. This involves looking at the context, culture, language, and literary style. "How does it apply to my life?" is the application stage. Here we are asking how the timeless truth of the passage applies to our lives today.

Let me give you an example. In John 3:16, we read, "For God so loved the world, that He gave His only begotten Son, that whoever believes in Him shall not perish, but have eternal life."

Observation: What does it say? God loved the world. He gave His only begotten Son. Whoever believes in Him shall not perish but have eternal life.

Interpretation: What does it mean? It means that God's love for humanity was so great that He gave His Son, Jesus, to die for our sins. Those who believe in Him will not face eternal separation from God but will have eternal life with Him.

Application: How does it apply to my life? It applies in that I can know and experience God's love personally by believing in Jesus. It also means that I am called to share this message of God's love with others.

Another example is found in Psalm 119:105: "Your word is a lamp to my feet And a light to my path."

Observation: God's Word is described as a lamp to our feet and a light to our path.

Interpretation: The psalmist is saying that God's Word provides guidance and direction in life.

Application: I can trust God's Word to guide me in the decisions I make and the paths I take in life.

As you can see, these three simple questions can open up the meaning of Scripture and help us to apply it in practical ways. The Bible is not meant to be a closed book. It is meant to be opened, read, and lived.

One of the best habits you can develop as a follower of Christ is daily Bible reading. It does not have to be long, but it should be consistent. Start with a few verses or a chapter a day. Read with an open heart and a willingness to be taught. Pray before you read, asking God to give you wisdom and understanding. Reflect on what you have read and how it applies to your life.

There was a time in my life when the Bible seemed like a closed book. It was confusing and hard to understand. But as I began to pray in faith for wisdom and understanding and as I developed the habit of daily reading, the Bible came alive to me. It was no longer just words on a page but God's living Word speaking to my heart. Hebrews 4:12 tells us, "For the word of God is living and active and sharper than any two-edged sword, and piercing as far as the division of soul and spirit, of both joints and marrow, and able to judge the thoughts and intentions of the heart."

When you approach the Bible with an open heart, a prayerful spirit, and a desire to know God, you will find that it is indeed living and active. It will guide you, correct you, encourage you, and transform you.

As important as it is to read the Bible with understanding, simply reading is not enough. God's Word is meant to settle deeply within us, shaping our thoughts, desires, and actions. The next step in our journey is to learn how to meditate on God's Word in a way that allows its truths to take root in our hearts and transform our lives.

Meditate God's Way

Now that we have been introduced to controlling what we allow into our minds, how to pray in faith for wisdom and understanding, and how to read the Bible in a simple manner, we need to talk about how to meditate on what we have read in the Bible.

"But prove yourselves doers of the word, and not merely hearers who delude themselves. For if anyone is a hearer of the word and not a doer, he is like a man who looks at his natural face in a mirror; for once he has looked at himself and gone away, he has immediately forgotten what kind of person he was" (Jas. 1:22-24, NASB).

For years, I was deluded with hearing but not doing the Word. I would read the Bible, but there was extraordinarily little, if any, substantial change in my life. Like James described, I would gain knowledge about the Bible but not apply it effectively. I often wondered why. Like I shared earlier in this book, I attended Bible college and seminary seeking an experiential relationship with Christ, but what I got was intellectual knowledge about the Bible. Since then, I have learned that it does not matter how much intellectual knowledge of the Bible I have. Intellectual knowledge of the Bible does not necessarily change the heart any more than knowing about the engineering behind the workings of a combustion engine will show me how to drive a car effectively. There is a difference between knowing about something and experiencing something. The question we must ask is, "How do we move from intellectual to experiential?"

Can we skip the intellectual and jump right into experiential? Not necessarily. We must have a little intellectual to understand experiential, but we do not have to have exhaustive intellectual to gain experiential. In fact, through experiential learning, we gain a better understanding of intellectual. By this I mean that, in a sense, intellectual is largely based on theory, but once experienced, the theory either proves to be true or false, through which we gain experiential knowledge. The problem is that often we are not inclined to move into experiential unless we are motivated by intellectual theory.

For example, let us say you have never tasted water. You can study water in books, learn its chemical makeup, and even listen to experts describe what it is like. You may imagine its coolness or the way it might quench thirst. But until you actually drink water, all you have is intellectual knowledge and imagination. Once you taste it, you move from imagination and theory into experience. At that point, you no longer just know about water—you know water.

The same is true with God's Word. Many people stop at imagination or intellectual knowledge. They read, they hear sermons, they study, but they never step into the realm of experience. Meditation is the bridge that takes us from simply knowing about God's Word to actually experiencing its reality.

Meditation is not emptying the mind as some Eastern philosophies teach, nor is it mindless repetition. Biblical meditation is filling the mind with God's Word, turning it over and over in your thoughts, picturing it, praying it, and letting it sink deep into your heart. It is the process by which truth moves from the head to the heart, from information to transformation.

Joshua 1:8 gives us a powerful picture of biblical meditation: "This book of the law shall not depart from your mouth, but you shall meditate on it day and night, so that you may be careful to do according to all that is written in it; for then you will make your way prosperous, and then you will have success." Notice that meditation leads to obedience, and obedience leads to prosperity and success as God defines it.

When we meditate on God's Word, we are not merely reading it; we are absorbing it, internalizing it, and allowing it to shape the way we think and live. Meditation involves slowing down, lingering over a passage, repeating it to ourselves, and asking the Holy Spirit to illuminate its meaning. It is allowing God's Word to speak to us personally and practically.

In my own life, I have discovered that the times I have truly grown in my walk with God were the times I consistently meditated on His Word. Reading gave me knowledge, but meditation brought transformation. It was in meditation that the verses I had read many times suddenly came alive with fresh meaning.

The practice of meditation is simple but profound. Set aside a quiet time. Take a short passage of Scripture. Read it slowly. Repeat it. Picture it. Pray it back to God. Ask how it applies to your life. Then carry it with you throughout the day, recalling it often and letting it sink deeper into your soul.

When meditation becomes a habit, you will find that God's Word begins to saturate your thoughts, influence your decisions, and guide your actions. You will experience the truth of Psalm 1:2-3: "But his delight is in the law of the Lord, and in His law he meditates day and night. He will be like a tree firmly planted by streams of water, which yields its fruit in its season, and its leaf does not wither; And in whatever he does, he prospers."

Meditation is God's way of moving us from knowledge to transformation, from hearing the Word to doing the Word. It is the means by which the truth of Scripture becomes living and active in us, producing lasting change and bearing fruit for God's glory.

As God's Word takes root in our hearts through meditation, it naturally overflows into our lives. What begins in private reflection is meant to bear fruit in public expression. The truths we have prayed over, read, and meditated upon are not just for our benefit alone—they are also for the encouragement and building up of others. In the next section, we will consider how to share what we have learned with those around us in a way that is simple, genuine, and effective.

Share Your Faith

In summary, we need to move from hearers of the Word to doers of the Word of God. The problem is that the world system has used every medium available to hijack our imaginations and plant negative thoughts and ideas about who God is, how we view ourselves, and how we view others. I have recommended that we take control of our minds and imaginations by controlling what we allow into our minds and then begin detoxing our minds from the damaging thoughts and negative self-talk by taking them captive and retraining the mind through meditating on the Word of God and practicing affirming biblical truths. If you will do these things, you will soon discover victory over the sins which so easily entangle you.

One of the ways that really helped me to solidify the biblical truths I have meditated on and began to verbally affirm is sharing those truths with others. In the following, I will explain a simple and effective manner to share the biblical truths you have discovered.

One of the most difficult things for a believer in Christ to do is share their faith. There are lots of reasons why, but the main reasons are that many do not know where to start, and many others are fearful of confrontation, so they just hope that they can show Christ silently in their social interactions. However, the problem, as we have discussed earlier, is that most Christians are not demonstrating the God-shaped life in their social interactions. In this section, I am going to share with you a simple but effective way of sharing your faith without being confrontational or sounding judgmental.

First, though, I would like to share with you some of my past experiences in sharing my own faith. In the early years of my faith journey, the way I shared my faith was confrontational and often judgmental. I thought it was my duty to point out people's sins and tell them they needed Jesus. This approach often ended with people being turned off, and I walked away feeling discouraged. Over time, God showed me a better way: to share my story.

When I tell my story, I simply share three things: who I was before Christ, what God did for me, and who I am now. This is not threatening, not judgmental, and very effective. People tend to listen to a story more than they listen to a lecture. A story disarms defensiveness and opens the door for genuine conversation.

As you could hopefully see from my own story, I shared about who I was, what Jesus did for me, and who I am now. I just evangelized you in a nonthreatening and nonjudgmental way. This is the best and most effective way to evangelize.

Another thing I would recommend is that you pray for those you are seeking to share your faith with. Typically, I pray Ephesians 3:14-21 in the following manner:

"For this reason I bow my knees before the Father, from whom every family in heaven and on earth derives its name, that He would grant you, according to the riches of His glory, to be strengthened with power through His Spirit in the inner man, so that Christ may dwell in your hearts through faith; and that you, being rooted and grounded in love, may be able to comprehend with all the saints what is the breadth and length and height and depth, and to know the love of Christ which surpasses knowledge, that you may be filled up to all the fullness of God. Now to Him who is able to do far more abundantly beyond all that we ask or think, according to the power that works within us, to Him be the glory in the church and in Christ Jesus to all generations forever and ever. Amen" (Eph. 3:14-21).

What I do is I fill in somebody's name in place of the "you" and "your." So, for example: "God, I pray that you would grant Shane, according to the riches of your glory, to be strengthened with power through your Spirit in Shane's inner being, so that Christ may dwell in Shane's heart through faith; and that Shane could be rooted and grounded in love, and be able to comprehend with all the saints what is the breadth and length and height and depth and to know your love for him which surpasses comprehension so that Shane could be filled up with the fullness of you. Lord, you are able to do far more beyond all that I could ask or think, so let Shane's salvation be glorious to you as he becomes a member of your church and testifies of you forever, amen!"

I believe God would answer prayers of that nature. Once you start praying a prayer like this for the person you are seeking to minister to, you can be confident that the Holy Spirit is working in their life and preparing them to respond to your story. Next, pray for an opportunity to share your story with those whom you have been praying for. I have learned to listen to other people and what is important to them before sharing my story with them. If you can, and if you do not already, get to know the person whom you desire to share your faith with. People are more inclined to listen to your story with sincere interest if they feel that you have a sincere interest in them. Rejoice with them when they decide to follow Jesus and commit to helping them grow in their understanding of who God is, who they are as new creations in Christ, and how to love others altruistically.

In summary, it is difficult for the average believer to share their faith for multiple reasons. Those who seek to share their faith through social interactions are not effectively winning souls, primarily because most Christians are no different morally than those they are attempting to win over with their social example. A Calvinistic understanding of salvation has spread through nearly all of Christian salvation doctrine, making the most common form of modern-day evangelism judgmental, unloving, and presenting false God concepts, which incite fear. The best form of evangelism is praying for the person you seek to minister to and then sharing with them your story, which should be something along the lines of: this is who I was, this is what God did for me, and this is who I am now.

As we have walked through these practical steps—controlling our thoughts, praying in faith, reading and meditating on Scripture, and sharing with others—we begin to see the outline of the God-shaped life take form. Yet this is not the end of the journey; it is the beginning of a lifelong pursuit of knowing God more fully and living in the fullness of His design. In the conclusion, we will step back and reflect on the larger picture, tying together the truths we have explored and pointing forward to the hope and purpose God offers to all who walk in His way.

Conclusion

Modern Christianity is in a moral dilemma where most professing believers in Christ are statistically no different in their behavior than the rest of the world. This is a direct result of the fact that most Christians have a distorted view of God, poor self-images, and corrupted ideas of others. Because how we view God affects every aspect of our lives, it is no wonder most believers struggle with moral purity.

The problem of distorted ideas about God, self, and others began with Adam and Eve, where a genetic change was introduced into mankind's gene pool and affected everyone born since. The resulting mind distortions affected our parents, who have an influence on our developing views of God, self, and others. Then, as we are exposed to culture, more corrupted ideas are presented about God, ourselves, and others. Media, a major culture player, has a huge influence over our imaginations and belief systems, which leads us even further away from truths about God, self, and others. Lastly, the religions we are exposed to lay down interpretive grids for how we read and understand our Bibles and ultimately affect how we view God, self, and others.

Beyond moral decay, holding distorted views of God, self, and others affects our mental and physical health in ways that would surprise most of us. Additionally, distorted views of God, self, and others impact the health of our social interactions and, not surprisingly, our spiritual well-being as well.

In the Bible, God reveals Himself to be a loving, benevolent creator who is in pursuit of His wayward creation and has afforded those who put their faith in Jesus Christ to be blessed with every spiritual blessing. One aspect of our spiritual blessings is the fact that we are new creations in Christ, which should improve our self-images. Another spiritual blessing is the ability to view and love others through God's lens of love, which greatly improves our social interaction.

To help restore our views of God, self, and others, I have suggested the following practices: begin by controlling what you allow into your mind or through your other senses, and take every thought captive to prevent the enemy from erecting strongholds in your thoughts and imagination. Then pray in faith for wisdom and understanding, followed by reading the Bible in the suggested simple manner. Next, meditate on what the Bible has revealed using the method suggested. Lastly, follow the simple plan of communicating your faith by sharing your story about how God has changed your life.

My hope is that as you put these practices into action, you will come to see God as He truly is—a loving Father who has blessed you with every spiritual blessing in Christ. As you embrace your new identity as His child and learn to love others with His kind of love, your life will reflect His design in ways that bring Him glory and bring you peace. The journey is not about perfection but about walking daily in the reality of who God is and who you are in Him. May you be encouraged to continue growing, to keep your gaze fixed on Him, and to live each day with the confidence that He is shaping your life for His eternal purpose.

These practices open the door to discovering and living God's divine blueprint. Yet they are not meant to be short-lived disciplines but lifelong habits that keep us rooted in God's truth and love. As we conclude this book, let us consider how to carry these truths forward in daily life, embracing the God-shaped life as an ongoing journey of transformation.

Chapter Five Reflection & Discussion Guide

For personal journaling, small group dialogue, or ministry training

Personal Reflection

1. Which of the practices in this chapter—controlling your gaze, prayer, Scripture reading, meditation, or sharing your faith—do you find most natural, and which is hardest for you?
2. How has focusing your attention shaped your thoughts and attitudes recently?
3. What role does prayer play in renewing your view of God, yourself, and others?

Bible Engagement

1. Read **Colossians 3:1–2**. How does Paul describe setting your mind on things above, and how does this connect with controlling your gaze?
2. Reflect on **Philippians 4:6–7**. How does prayer with thanksgiving change the way you experience God's peace?
3. Read **Psalm 1:1–3**. What picture does the psalmist give of a life rooted in God's Word, and how does this connect to meditation?

Group Discussion

1. How have you seen God use practical disciplines—prayer, Scripture, meditation, or testimony—to reshape people's lives?
2. What steps can we take together to encourage one another to keep our minds fixed on God's truth?

3. In what ways does sharing your faith not only bless others but also strengthen your own walk with Christ?

Want to go deeper?

Download the free companion journal at 180perspective.com/the-God-shaped-life-study for extended prompts, prayers, and space to reflect.

Chapter Six: Living the God-Shaped Life

Living the God-shaped life is not a one-time event or a spiritual quick fix. It is a journey of daily surrender, a walk of faith that continues until the day we see Jesus face to face. Transformation becomes real the moment we place our trust in Christ, but living in the reality of that transformation requires perseverance, as we renew our minds to be more in line with the reality of who we are as new creations in Christ and citizens of God's kingdom. Scripture reminds us to run the race with endurance, fixing our eyes on Jesus, the pioneer and perfecter of our faith (Heb. 12:1–2). That means this life is not a sprint but a marathon. There will be days when progress feels slow, and there will be setbacks, but maturity does not come through perfection. It comes through the steady rhythm of faithfulness, choosing again and again to walk with Christ.

Yet even as we walk this path, we quickly discover there are obstacles. Old thought patterns try to creep back in, whispering the same lies that once held us captive. Sometimes we do things or act in ways that are outside of God's design and purpose; that is how sin is defined—a missing of the mark, like shooting an arrow and missing the target. The cunning enemy of your soul is quick to attack your mind when you miss the mark with deceptive lies about your identity: *"You are no good. God hasn't changed you!"* Soon guilt and shame begin to settle in, and if left unchecked, they can warp the way you see yourself. A distorted self-image takes root.

Like Adam and Eve, we hide from God, convinced that our failure has ruined the relationship. We think, *Why would God want anything to do with me after I've failed Him again? He must hate me for what I've done.* The enemy waits for such moments, eager to drag us further down a path of despair—the same path that Cain walked when resentment and lies took root in his heart. Scripture warns of those who "went the way of Cain," allowing jealousy, anger, and rebellion to turn them away from God's truth (Jude 1:11).

But you must remember, your missing the mark does nothing to change God's love for you. You can't sin or fail enough to outdo His love. That's why Paul calls it "a love that surpasses knowledge" (Eph. 3:19). In reality, God is the Father of the wayward, constantly scanning the horizon like in Jesus' parable of the prodigal son—looking down the road with anticipation that you will come home. And when you do, He doesn't scold or shame you; He throws a celebration like no other.

You are always welcome at God's table, no matter how far you've wandered or how often you've missed the mark. This is why Jesus came—to seek and to save the lost, just as the shepherd leaves the ninety-nine to go after the one sheep that has strayed. Such is the relentless pursuit of God's love.

So no, you can't push God away or exhaust His grace. But you *can* let the enemy deceive you into believing otherwise. He will whisper that you are not worthy, that you are damaged goods, that you'll never measure up. And when those lies take hold, a wounded self-image drives you into hiding, crouching behind the same bushes where Adam and Eve once tried to cover their shame. All the while, Jesus is calling your name, inviting you out of hiding into the light of His love.

124

That is why it matters what we allow into our minds. The enemy's oldest tactic is still deception, but today his voice often comes through the flood of media surrounding us. He has taken hold of much of it, turning it into a weapon to plant lies and raise up strongholds in the minds of the unsuspecting. Hour after hour, images, messages, and stories pour into our hearts, shaping our view of God, distorting our self-image, and twisting how we see others. If left unguarded, these influences weaken faith and dull the truth of God's Word.

This is why Scripture tells us to "take captive every thought to make it obedient to Christ" (2 Cor. 10:5). We can't stop the noise of the world, but we can choose what we allow to take root in our minds. Just as the psalmist prayed, "Turn my eyes from worthless things; preserve my life according to your word" (Ps. 119:37), so must we learn to turn our gaze away from what corrupts and fix it again on the Lord. By guarding what enters through our eyes and ears, we strengthen our faith and give God's truth room to reshape how we see Him, ourselves, and others.

This is especially important because, as I pointed out at the beginning of this book, many churches have lost sight of what true community should look like. Too often, we see hypocrisy and empty religion, a body that reflects the world more than Christ. But when our minds are renewed, and our lives are aligned with God's design, the church becomes what it was always meant to be—a family that grows together in love, helping one another stand firm in the truth and pulling each other forward into maturity.

When the battle for the mind feels overwhelming, God has also given us the gift of community. We were never meant to fight alone. Walking with Christ is a shared journey where brothers and sisters help one another stand firm when the enemy's lies press in. Within the body of Christ, we find encouragement, correction, and the reminder that we are not who the world says we are, nor who the enemy accuses us of being—we are children of God. Paul wrote that the body "grows and builds itself up in love, as each part does its work" (Eph. 4:16). Your growth strengthens others, and their growth strengthens you. That is how the family of God was designed to function, pulling one another forward into maturity.

And even when the road feels long, we do not walk it in our own strength. God Himself is faithful. He has promised that the good work He began in us will be carried on to completion until the day of Christ Jesus (Phil. 1:6). That promise should steady us with hope. Growth may feel slow, but it is real. We are not striving to prove ourselves or to manufacture change; we are learning to live in the reality of who we already are in Christ. Each stumble becomes another chance to experience His mercy, and each step of obedience becomes another marker of His transforming grace at work within us.

To live the God-shaped life, we return again and again to the rhythms that keep us aligned with His truth. Each day we set our gaze on Christ, refusing to let our thoughts be captured by the enemy's lies. We pray in faith, asking for wisdom and strength to see things as God sees them. We open the Scriptures—not as a duty to be checked off, but as the living Word that renews our minds and reminds us of who we are in Him. And we meditate on what He reveals, letting His truth settle deeply in our hearts.

These rhythms continue as we gather weekly with other believers to worship, encourage one another, and rest in God's presence. Over a lifetime, we learn to share our faith by telling our own story of how God has changed us, discipling others who walk the path behind us, and loving as Christ loved us. Paul's words remind us of this reality: "Let the message of Christ dwell among you richly… and whatever you do, whether in word or deed, do it all in the name of the Lord Jesus" (Col. 3:16–17).

At the beginning of this book, I spoke of the church's moral dilemma—how too often we appear no different from the world, and how hypocrisy empties our witness of love and power. That is where we began: identifying the problem of distorted views of God, self, and others. But now we end with hope, because the God-shaped life offers a better way.

Through Christ, we have been given every spiritual blessing. We are new creations, adopted as children of God and called to see ourselves and others through His love. When we live in this reality—renewing our minds, guarding our hearts, and choosing the rhythms that anchor us in His truth—we become the church God intended: a people whose lives reflect His design, who build one another up in love, and who shine as light in a world desperate for hope.

The journey is not about achieving perfection, but about walking daily with our eyes fixed on Jesus. As we do, our lives testify that God is who He says He is, and that His love is stronger than every lie of the enemy. This is the vision that began in Eden, was redeemed at the cross, and is now lived out in you and me—the God-shaped life, bringing glory to Him and peace to our souls.

Conclusion

Throughout this journey, we have uncovered how distorted views of God, ourselves, and others can take root through family, culture, media, and religion. We have seen the painful consequences of these distortions—spiritual confusion, emotional wounds, strained relationships, and even physical harm. Yet in every chapter, God's truth has spoken a better word.

Scripture reveals a God of love who has made us new in Christ and calls us to live in His light. We are no longer bound by false images or destructive patterns—we are children of God, set free to love and to live out His design. Through prayer, the renewing of our minds, immersion in His Word, and the daily practice of walking with Him, we learn to align our lives with the reality of who He is and who we are in Him.

But this is not the end of the journey. It is an invitation to begin again each day, choosing to let God shape your life rather than the influences of the world. The God-shaped life is not about perfection—it is about transformation. It is about seeing God rightly, seeing yourself as His beloved child, and seeing others through His eyes of love.

My prayer is that you will not only understand these truths but live them out. Let this book serve as a launching point, a reminder that God's design for your life is good, His love is sure, and His Spirit is at work within you. Step into the freedom, hope, and wholeness He offers. The God-shaped life is waiting—embrace it fully and let your life reflect His glory.

May God guide you in the power of the Holy Spirit!

In Christ, Steve

Chapter Six Reflection & Discussion Guide

For personal journaling, small group dialogue, or ministry training

Personal Reflection

1. Looking back over this book, what has changed most in your view of God?
2. How has your understanding of yourself as a new creation in Christ and a citizen of God's kingdom shaped the way you see your life today?
3. What lies from the enemy about your identity have you most needed to confront, and how has God's truth spoken into them?

Bible Engagement

1. Read **Hebrews 12:1–2**. How does "fixing our eyes on Jesus" give you strength to persevere when progress feels slow?
2. Reflect on **2 Corinthians 10:5**. What does it mean to take every thought captive to Christ, and how can this reshape what you allow into your mind through media and culture?
3. Read **Philippians 1:6**. How does God's promise to complete the work He began in you give you hope for the journey ahead?

Group Discussion

1. How can the church move from the hypocrisy and distortion described at the start of this book to the picture of community described here in Chapter Six?
2. What rhythms—daily, weekly, and lifelong—can we practice together as a community to help one another live the God-shaped life?
3. In what ways can your group or church shine more brightly as a people who reflect God's love to a watching world?

Want to go deeper?

Download the free companion journal at 180perspective.com/the-God-shaped-life-study for extended prompts, prayers, and space to reflect.

Bibliography

Armstrong, Kim. "The Power of Culture." *Observer Magazine* 18, no. 5 (2005): 15–18.

Barna Group. *The Impact of Family on Identity Formation.* Ventura, CA: Barna Group, 2017.

Barna, George. Interview by *Homiletics Online*, April 2000.

Bauer, Walter, Frederick William Danker, William F. Arndt, and F. Wilbur Gingrich. *A Greek-English Lexicon of the New Testament and Other Early Christian Literature.* 3rd ed. Chicago: University of Chicago Press, 2000.

Bouchard, Thomas J., Jr., et al. "Genetic and Environmental Influences on Mental Health and Religious Interests: A Twin Study." *Journal of Personality* 69, no. 6 (2001): 931–952.

Bright, Bill. *The Journey Home.* Orlando: NewLife, 1995.

Bruce, F. F. *The Epistle to the Hebrews.* Rev. ed. Grand Rapids, MI: Eerdmans, 1990.

Carson, D. A. *The Gospel According to John.* Grand Rapids, MI: Eerdmans, 1991.

Fingelkurts, Alexander A., and Andrew A. Fingelkurts. "Is Our Brain Hardwired to Produce God, or Is Our Brain Hardwired to Perceive God?" *Cognitive Processing* 10, no. 1 (2009): 13–29.

Flemming, Dean. Contextualization in the New Testament: Patterns for Theology and Mission. Downers Grove, IL: InterVarsity Press, 2005.

Froese, Paul, and Christopher Bader. *America's Four Gods: What We Say About God—and What That Says About Us*. New York: Oxford University Press, 2010.

Geisler, Norman. *Systematic Theology*. Minneapolis: Bethany House, 2002.

Goethe, Johann Wolfgang von. Quoted in Emil Ludwig. *Goethe: The History of a Man*. New York: G. P. Putnam's Sons, 1928.

Garnets, Linda. "Sexual Orientations in Perspective." *Cultural Diversity and Ethnic Minority Psychology* 8, no. 2 (2002): 115–129.

Guthrie, Donald. *The Letter to the Hebrews*. Grand Rapids, MI: Eerdmans, 1983.

Harlow, Harry F. "The Nature of Love." *American Psychologist* 13, no. 12 (1958): 673–685.

Huffington Post. "Americans and Bible Reading." 2013.

Jennings, Timothy R. The God-Shaped Brain: How Changing Your View of God Transforms Your Life. Downers Grove, IL: InterVarsity Press, 2013.

Jones, E. Stanley. The Christ of the Mount: A Working Philosophy of Life. Nashville: Abingdon, 1931.

Leaf, Caroline. *Switch On Your Brain*. Grand Rapids, MI: Baker Books, 2013.

Martin. "How TV Affects Your Brain Functions." *Erupting Mind*, 2009. https://www.eruptingmind.com/how-tv-affects-your-brain/